Opening
PAUL'S LETTERS

Opening
PAUL'S LETTERS

A READER'S GUIDE
TO GENRE AND
INTERPRETATION

Patrick Gray

Baker Academic
a division of Baker Publishing Group
Grand Rapids, Michigan

Published by Baker Academic
a division of Baker Publishing Group
PO Box 6287, Grand Rapids, MI 49516-6287
www.bakeracademic.com

Printed in the United States of America

Library of Congress Cataloging-in-Publication Data
Gray, Patrick, 1970–
    Opening Paul's letters : a reader's guide to genre and interpretation / Patrick Gray.
        p.   cm.
    Includes bibliographical references and index.
    ISBN 978-0-8010-3922-5 (pbk.)
    1. Bible. N.T. Epistles of Paul—Criticism, interpretation, etc. 2. Bible. N.T. Epistles of Paul—Hermeneutics. I. Title.
    BS2650.52.G73 2012
    227′.06—dc23   2011030807

In keeping with biblical principles of creation stewardship, Baker Publishing Group advocates the responsible use of our natural resources. As a member of the Green Press Initiative, our company uses recycled paper when possible. The text paper of this book is composed in part of post-consumer waste.

Contents

Contents

Preface

B ooks about the apostle Paul could easily fill a small library. No single work can adequately address the range of questions raised by his letters, and the present volume is no exception. Other volumes provide historical overviews of Paul's life and ministry, commentary on the individual letters, or surveys of his theology. Interest in these topics is what motivates most people to read his letters in the first place. The premise of this book is that before readers can be in a position to appreciate Paul and his theology, they must understand something very basic about his writings: they are letters. And they must understand what letters were and how they functioned in Paul's first-century setting.

In the pages that follow, the primary focus is therefore on the literary genre of Paul's writings. It is sometimes easy to forget that reading the New Testament is, by and large, an exercise in reading other people's mail. Paul wrote and sent more of this "mail" than anyone else. To read his letters as they were meant to be read, it is necessary to be familiar with ancient letter genres. Letters in ancient Greece and Rome are in some ways similar to modern letters but also differ in key respects. My aim here is to orient readers to these similarities and differences, to highlight the ways in which Paul adheres to and departs from established conventions in his letters, and to outline strategies for making sense of them.

A number of individuals deserve recognition for their assistance along the way. My colleague Steve McKenzie first suggested writing a book on Paul that would model an approach to Paul and equip students to read and interpret his letters. His book *How to Read the Bible: History, Prophecy, Literature—Why Modern Readers Need to Know the Difference and What It Means for Faith Today* (New York: Oxford University Press, 2005) is an excellent resource that does for the entire Bible what I have attempted to do for Paul. Steve's comments as I have written these chapters have been immensely helpful. The editors at Baker, Jim Kinney and James Ernest, also provided expert guidance as I prepared the manuscript for publication. To Rhodes College I also owe a debt of gratitude, not only for the generous support provided by the administration in the form of a faculty development grant but also for the privilege of teaching the outstanding students who come here. Finally, I am forever thankful to Alex, Lily, Joseph, and Dominic for their love and encouragement.

Abbreviations

General

BCE	before the Common Era
CE	Common Era
KJV	King James Version
NRSV	New Revised Standard Version

Old Testament

Gen.	Genesis
Exod.	Exodus
Lev.	Leviticus
Num.	Numbers
Deut.	Deuteronomy
Josh.	Joshua
Judg.	Judges
Ruth	Ruth
1–2 Sam.	1–2 Samuel
1–2 Kings	1–2 Kings
1–2 Chron.	1–2 Chronicles
Ezra	Ezra
Neh.	Nehemiah
Esther	Esther
Job	Job
Ps(s).	Psalm(s)
Prov.	Proverbs

Eccles.	Ecclesiastes
Song	Song of Songs
Isa.	Isaiah
Jer.	Jeremiah
Lam.	Lamentations
Ezek.	Ezekiel
Dan.	Daniel
Hosea	Hosea
Joel	Joel
Amos	Amos
Obad.	Obadiah
Jon.	Jonah
Mic.	Micah
Nah.	Nahum
Hab.	Habakkuk
Zeph.	Zephaniah
Hag.	Haggai
Zech.	Zechariah
Mal.	Malachi

New Testament

Matt.	Matthew
Mark	Mark
Luke	Luke
John	John
Acts	Acts

Rom.	Romans	Titus	Titus
1–2 Cor.	1–2 Corinthians	Philem.	Philemon
Gal.	Galatians	Heb.	Hebrews
Eph.	Ephesians	James	James
Phil.	Philippians	1–2 Pet.	1–2 Peter
Col.	Colossians	1–3 John	1–3 John
1–2 Thess.	1–2 Thessalonians	Jude	Jude
1–2 Tim.	1–2 Timothy	Rev.	Revelation

Introduction

❉

T he first book I bought and read when I entered college bore
the title *How to Read a Book*. It was required reading for a
seminar taken by all freshmen, many of whom felt insulted,
not so much by the author, Mortimer J. Adler, as by the professors who
had assigned it. Maybe other people need such a book, we reasoned,
but not us. After all, how could we have gained admission to college
if we were unable to read a book? When the seminar concluded, a
fraternity threw a book-burning party to which anyone with a copy
of Adler was invited. It was very well attended.

Despite the offense we took at the suggestion that we might have
something to learn about reading books, as we worked through Aristotle, Marx, Dostoyevsky, and Hemingway, in addition to textbooks
for courses in biology, economics, and calculus and surveys of Japanese
history and American politics, we begrudgingly conceded that Adler
had a point. There is much more to reading than simply deciphering
black marks on a white page. Different kinds of books have different aims and demand different approaches. Just as it is possible to
hear someone without really listening, it is possible to "read" a book
without really reading it.

This is a book about reading books. To be precise, it is a book
about reading texts that are usually called books, collected together
in a much larger book, the title of which—the Bible—comes from the

1

Greek word meaning "books" (*biblia*). But the books with which this volume is concerned—the letters of Paul the apostle—are not books in the ordinary sense. They are ancient letters, and recognizing the difference that this difference makes is the key to reading them well.

Reading and Interpretation

Another key to reading Paul's letters well—for that matter, to reading any text, ancient or modern, sacred or secular—is to realize that reading always means interpreting. "Interpretation" is of course a synonym for "translation." Readers of Paul's letters, which were originally written in Greek, often overlook that they are reading him secondhand, as it were. Anyone who has ever attempted to master a second language knows that things can change in translation. Some phrases and concepts cannot be adequately expressed in a foreign language. As the Italian proverb puts it, *traduttori traditori*, "translators are traitors."

But as crucial as it surely is to have a reliable translation, interpretation is much more than accurately rendering words in one language into another. Especially when it involves the Bible, people tend to think of interpretation as a standard or default mode in which to approach a text when it is hard to understand or its surface meaning is too fantastic or bizarre to be accepted. When a text presents no difficulties, one simply has to read it and not bother with interpreting it. Yet readers are constantly making interpretive decisions, even when they are not conscious of this fact. This becomes clear, as it turns out, when a text is not entirely clear. When something is unclear, we begin to ask questions. Interpretation is a process of framing appropriate questions about a text and then finding ways of answering those questions.

Take the following text as an example:

> Upon my bed at night
>   I sought him whom my soul loves;
> I sought him, but found him not;
>   I called him, but he gave no answer.
> "I will rise now and go about the city,
>   in the streets and in the squares;

> I will seek him whom my soul loves."
> I sought him, but found him not.
> The sentinels found me,
>   as they went about in the city.
> "Have you seen him whom my soul loves?"
> Scarcely had I passed them,
>   when I found him whom my soul loves.
> I held him, and would not let him go
>   until I brought him into my mother's house,
>   and into the chamber of her that conceived me.

What does one need to know in order to make sense of this passage? The list of relevant questions is virtually endless. The basic questions of the journalist may first come to mind. Who wrote it? When was it written? For whom was it written? What is the aim of the author in writing this? Is the author male or female? What kind of text is this? Is this the entire text or an excerpt? Is this an autobiographical report of actual events? Is it a report of a dream or a fantasy? In what language was it originally written, if not English? How was this message received? Are the author and the speaker in the passage the same person? Would the speaker be embarrassed by this message being read by someone other than the intended audience? Before one even attempts to answer these questions, it is not difficult to see what difference the answers might make. A reader might regard the paragraph as a touching excerpt from a woman's diary, but if the speaker is a man, the response might be quite different on both an emotional and intellectual level.

The passage quoted above comes from Song of Songs 3:1–4, a book included in the Old Testament. Does this furnish all the information necessary to make sense of the text? No, not exactly. In fact, it complicates matters even further in certain respects. Why is *this* in the Bible? It resembles erotic literature (even more so when one reads the rest of the Song of Songs), so should one assume that it is not meant to titillate but is instead allegorical in nature? If it is from the Song of Songs (also called the Song of Solomon), is Solomon really the author? Why would a king write this? Why would a man write this? Or is "Solomon" adopting a feminine persona for some literary purpose? If Solomon is not the author, why is someone else adopting a male pseudonym while simultaneously adopting a female persona in the text? Since this is in the Bible, which has provided spiritual guidance for centuries of readers, perhaps it would be appropriate to ask, "How should I live my life in light of what this text says?"

Consciously or unconsciously, every reader of every text is constantly asking and immediately answering questions in order to make sense of the text. It is difficult to make sense of a text if everything about it remains up in the air. Of all the possible questions one could pose to a text, some are more germane than others. Some are necessary for understanding, while others, however interesting, focus attention on peripheral matters. Still other questions may be entirely inappropriate for the text under consideration, though this may not become apparent until later in the process. Certain basic questions will apply to any and every text, but each text also elicits its own particular questions.

Approaches to Paul's letters vary according to the types of questions readers bring to them. It is possible to bring some sense of order to the bewildering variety of questions by dividing them into three categories. Questions about Paul's letters may focus on (1) "the world behind the text," (2) "the world of the text," and (3) "the world in front of the text."[1] "The world behind the text" refers to the historical, cultural, social, political, literary, and religious context of the flesh-and-blood author: What was Paul trying to say? What concrete conditions influenced the way Paul expressed himself? Who comprised his original audience? "The world of the text" refers to the literary, aesthetic, and structural characteristics of the author's work. This approach often applies to narrative works, with attention to plot and character, but it also applies to writings with rhetorical features, such as speeches or letters. The focus here is on the text, the whole text, and nothing but the text. "The world in front of the text" refers to what takes place when one reads, between the words on the page and the "real" readers who engage it: How have Paul's letters been read throughout history? What factors influence readers as they interpret the letters? How do they inspire the reader? How do different readers

1. The categories are those of Paul Ricoeur, *Hermeneutics and the Human Sciences*, ed. and trans. John B. Thompson (Cambridge: Cambridge University Press, 1981), 141–44.

respond to Paul's teachings? How *should* different readers respond to Paul's teachings? How have the letters shaped history and society in the centuries since they first appeared?

Readers may ask questions focusing on any of these three different "worlds" when interpreting any given text. A passage from one of Paul's letters to the Corinthians (1 Cor. 11:23–26) is sufficiently rich to sustain close scrutiny from multiple angles. In commenting on disputes about their behavior when they come together to share a meal, he connects their circumstances to the last meal shared by Jesus with his disciples:

> For I received from the Lord what I also handed on to you, that the Lord Jesus on the night when he was betrayed took a loaf of bread, and when he had given thanks, he broke it and said, "This is my body that is for you. Do this in remembrance of me." In the same way he took the cup also, after supper, saying, "This cup is the new covenant in my blood. Do this, as often as you drink it, in remembrance of me." For as often as you eat this bread and drink the cup, you proclaim the Lord's death until he comes.

Readers stand "in front of" the text, so one might begin with questions from that angle: Are "we" the "you" who "proclaim the Lord's death until he comes"? Should Christians commemorate this ritual on a weekly (daily? monthly? quarterly?) basis? How do Catholics and Protestants interpret this passage? One might ignore such contemporary concerns and focus on the world "of" the text: How does the anecdote related here support the larger argument? Does it interrupt the flow of the passage? Going back further, "behind" the text, other questions arise: Why does Paul think this reference is relevant to the situation he is discussing? Are the Corinthians already familiar with this tradition about Jesus? Did Jesus really say what Paul reports him saying? Is Jesus speaking literally or figuratively when he says, "This is my body"? (It would appear to depend on what the meaning of "is" is.)

How to answer the last question raises an issue that is important when thinking about how to read Paul's letters. Jesus's statement is ambiguous. It is very difficult, if not impossible, to know with certainty what Jesus meant. This is not unusual when an author is not available to explain. Perhaps, as many have said in connection with this and other contested questions, "it just depends on the reader." Different readers—Protestants and Catholics, for instance—undeniably come away from the text having understood it in different ways, and these differences normally correspond to the religious commitments and presuppositions of the reader. But these commitments and presuppositions originally derive, at some historical point, from different readings of the text; therefore, it is circular to try to close the question by invoking the conflicting biases of different readers. While contextual clues point in the direction of one reading or the other, at such a distance it will perhaps be impossible to settle the question once and for all. But that is not the same as saying that "it just depends on the reader." If it were possible to ask Jesus or Paul whether we should read "this is my body" literally or figuratively, a moment's reflection makes it obvious that Jesus probably would not say, "It doesn't really matter what I think. I wasn't really trying to say anything specific," and that Paul probably would not say, "It means whatever you want it to mean."[2]

Paul's letters are filled with obscure, ambiguous, and confusing statements. He does not always meet the standard established by Gregory of Nazianzus in the fourth century when he says that letters should be "understood at once" and should require no interpretation (*Epistle* 51.4). What does Paul mean, exactly, when he says that women who prophesy in a church setting should always wear a veil "because of the angels" (1 Cor. 11:10)? Or when he compares the second coming of Christ to "a thief in the night" and the onset of "labor pains [for] a pregnant woman" (1 Thess. 5:2–3)? Does he really mean it when he says that "everyone" who simply "calls on the name of the Lord shall be saved" (Rom. 10:13)? Or when he tells the Galatians, "I

---

2. Martin Luther made this point in his debate with fellow reformer Ulrich Zwingli over the doctrine of transubstantiation. While Luther rejected the doctrine, he was not quite willing to say that Jesus might not have meant what he seems to have said. Zwingli declared that "is" in this instance meant "symbolizes." Luther cried foul; following this arbitrary method of interpretation, he argued, "God" might mean "cuckoo," "created" might mean "ate," and "heavens and earth" might mean "hedgehog." The first verse of the Bible would then mean, "The cuckoo ate the hedgehog" (quoted in William Placher, *A History of Christian Theology: An Introduction* [Philadelphia: Westminster, 1983], 190). As Alice tells Humpty Dumpty in *Through the Looking-Glass*, one cannot make a text mean anything one likes.

wish those who unsettle you would castrate themselves" (Gal. 5:12)? Does he believe that "women should be silent in the churches" (1 Cor. 14:34), or has this command been inserted into the text by a later scribe? Does Paul believe that the Old Testament and the New Testament present two separate and opposed gods, as the second-century teacher Marcion interpreted 2 Cor. 4:4 ("the god of this world has blinded the minds of the unbelievers, to keep them from seeing the light of the gospel"), or does he believe there is only one God? To be sure, interpretations depend on the interpreter. Meaning, however, is a different matter. It is possible to treat Paul's letters like picnics or potluck dinners to which the author brings the words and the reader brings the meanings.[3] But is that the best way to read them? If one distinguishes between "what the text meant" in Paul's time and "what the text means" now, is it permissible for a text to "mean" what it never "meant" when it was originally written?[4] Should one operate in accordance with an interpretive Golden Rule: Interpret others as you would have others interpret you?

Questions attending to different aspects of Paul's letters (behind/of/ in front of the text) make different kinds of sense of them. This volume will focus on making sense of the letters by reading Paul as he wanted and expected to be read and understood, with only occasional forays into the world in front of the text. Discussion of Paul's relevance to present-day concerns is perfectly appropriate. Indeed, it is the main, or sometimes the only, reason many people still read his letters. But to focus too quickly or exclusively on the theological or ethical dimensions—by asking, for example, whether one is truly justified by faith (Gal. 3:24); or whether Paul was too pessimistic about human nature (Rom. 1:18–32; 5:12–14) or too optimistic about the capacity of human governments to carry out God's will (Rom. 13:1–7; Titus 3:1–2); or how to translate his teachings about equality (Gal. 3:28; Col. 3:11) for the purpose of improving contemporary race relations; or whether his attitudes about the role of women (Eph. 5:22–24) are

3. See E. D. Hirsch Jr., *Validity in Interpretation* (New Haven: Yale University Press, 1967), 1.
4. This distinction was popularized by Krister Stendahl, "Biblical Theology, Contemporary," in *The Interpreter's Dictionary of the Bible*, ed. G. A. Buttrick et al. (Nashville: Abingdon, 1962), 1:418–32.

binding for twenty-first-century Christians; or what churches have to learn from Paul about conducting their affairs (1 Cor. 5:6–13; 12:1–31; 1 Tim. 5:1–22); or whether Paul is worthy of imitation (1 Cor. 11:1; 2 Tim. 3:10–11)—is to put the proverbial cart before the horse. To answer such questions, it is incumbent on the interpreter to make a conscientious effort first to identify Paul's concerns and understand what he was trying to say in his own context. Whether the aim is to agree or to disagree with him, to apply his teachings or to undermine his authority, there is little point in reading Paul's letters if one has no interest in hearing Paul's voice.

Due to their special status as part of the Scriptures regarded as authoritative by hundreds of millions of Christians, it is easy to overlook the ways in which other texts present similar challenges. Comparison with the United States Constitution, for example, reveals a number of parallels. First, "we the people" expect both documents to speak to a host of issues that their authors never anticipated. Second, close reading reveals obscure statements and inconsistencies (real or apparent) in abundance, a reminder that neither text is self-interpreting. Third, readers attempt—often without success—to reconcile or account for these discrepancies. Fourth, readers pursue conflicting strategies for making sense of the texts as they have been passed down, sometimes privileging "original intent" and sometimes emphasizing that they are "living and breathing" documents. Fifth, valid interpretation must, in some manner, take prior discussion and precedent into account.

Many readers also overlook that making sense of the letters requires the same basic set of skills as making sense of other documents. Benjamin Jowett, an Oxford professor who had written books about Paul but was better known as an expert on Plato, made this point in an essay that sparked considerable controversy when it was published in 1860.[5] Interpret the Bible "like any other book" was Jowett's rule of thumb. Making sense of Paul entails asking many of the same questions that one asks when making sense of Sophocles or Shakespeare or Melville or Machiavelli.

---

5. Benjamin Jowett, "On the Interpretation of Scripture," in *Essays and Reviews*, 7th ed. (London: Longman, Green, Longman & Roberts, 1861), 330–433, esp. 377.

Reading Other People's Mail: The Importance of Genre

Foremost among the questions one must ask are those pertaining to literary genre. "Genre," like the Latin *genus* from which it derives, refers to a type or a category, whether of literature, music, art, or some other medium. Insofar as "the Bible" is not itself a literary genre, Jowett's principle requires a minor refinement. Paradoxically, to read the Bible "like any other book," one must recognize that it is *not* like any other book in the sense that it does not fall in a single genre but, rather, contains examples of several different genres. The genres represented in the Bible include poetry, short stories, historical narratives, prophecy, laws, parables, proverbs, genealogies—and letters. Of the twenty-seven books of the New Testament, twenty-one are letters, and two other books (Acts and Revelation) contain letters. Of these twenty-one letters, thirteen are attributed to Paul, another was for centuries regarded as a work of Paul (Hebrews), another mentions him by name (2 Peter), and another is widely considered a response to Paul's teachings (James).

Every literary genre has its distinguishing characteristics in terms of form and content. These rules may not be hard and fast, but they are sufficiently consistent that competent readers can tell one genre from another. Poetry in English often (but not always) rhymes. Topics treated in verse typically include love, death, and nature, but not economic policy or automotive maintenance. Country and western lyrics regularly mention trucks, trains, prison, and getting drunk. Newspaper stories are written at a fifth-grade level. Epics feature gods and heroes and begin *in medias res*, "in the middle of things." Comedies—in ancient Greece and Elizabethan England, at any rate—end in love and laughter, while tragedies end in death and destruction. Children's Bibles are full of pictures, especially of animals. High school textbooks usually include lists of terms, study questions, charts, and glossaries. Computer instruction manuals are meant to be concise and easy to understand but rarely seem so to those who might actually turn to them for help.

The familiarity of the conventions of various genres can be seen in the ease with which skilled writers are able to imitate them. Two examples illustrate the power that genre cues exert on readers. In 1835, a New York newspaper published a series of articles (presented as reprints from the *Edinburgh Journal of Science*) reporting the spectacular findings from a powerful telescope in South Africa, such as the existence on the moon of unicorns, men resembling bats, rivers, and a temple made from sapphires and rubies. The story was widely believed until it was revealed as a parody of the speculations of certain astronomers and theologians. The case of Alan Sokal, a physicist at New York University, is similar. In 1996, one of the preeminent journals devoted to postmodernist theory published an article by Sokal with the title "Transgressing the Boundaries: Towards a Transformative Hermeneutics of Quantum Gravity." It resembled most other articles in the journal, with copious footnotes, specialized jargon, obscure references, and impossibly dense prose, and its main thesis was that gravity, indeed all of physical reality, is "at bottom nothing more than a social and linguistic construct." Sokal, too, revealed that the piece was a parody of writings in a field that he considered intellectually sloppy. That either of these articles convinced so many readers that they were authentic despite their patently absurd content is a powerful testimony to the influence of genre in the shaping of reader expectations.

Identification of genre is absolutely essential when attempting to make sense of a text, and Paul's letters are no exception. Without an accurate grasp of the literary genre of a text, it is difficult to determine which questions to ask when trying to make sense of it. For example, it makes much more sense to inquire about the plot of a novel than of a letter. And the same question can have different meanings when posed to works in different genres. To ask whether a newspaper article is true is not the same as asking if a haiku or one of Aesop's fables is true. Once the genre is known, it is easier to gauge the relative importance of questions about the author's identity, purpose, and so forth. Genre constitutes the medium through which the author communicates with the audience. The expectations of the audience are crucial in this regard. When an audience discerns the genre, it knows which questions (as well as answers) are appropriate and which are not.

In most cases, the genre of a work is obvious. Most works do not explicitly identify their genre because it is not necessary. Errors may still occur, as when many listeners mistook Orson Welles's 1938 radio production of *The War of the Worlds* for a news report about an alien invasion, or when readers of Arthur Conan Doyle's stories send letters to Sherlock Holmes at 221B Baker Street in London, unaware that Holmes is a fictional character. On occasion, an author may, for whatever reason, intentionally blur the lines between different genres. Dan Brown's best-selling novel *The Da Vinci Code* caused a stir due to sensational claims it makes about Jesus, the Bible, and the history of Christianity. Although it is a work of fiction, on the page before the story opens, in bold capital letters he declares the "fact" that "all descriptions of artwork, architecture, documents, and secret rituals in the novel are accurate."[6] Many of his characters' descriptions of the Bible, however, are not remotely accurate. Has he simply done very shoddy research, or is Brown's declaration itself a part of the fiction that he hopes will make his characters' historical claims seem more plausible? Not all mistakes about genre are the result of deception or the cause of great confusion. Martin Luther King Jr.'s "Letter from Birmingham Jail" begins like a letter ("My dear fellow clergymen") and ends like a letter ("Yours for the cause of Peace and Brotherhood") but is really an essay meant for publication and was never sent to the eight ministers who had criticized his tactics as leader of the civil rights movement. The difference this makes to the message it conveys is negligible.

The potential for misunderstanding is multiplied when readers encounter literature from a different time and place. Because the Bible's influence is so pervasive, it is easy to forget that it was written long ago in a land far away and by authors formed by a culture that is alien to most of its modern readers. The cues that an ancient Judean would have readily recognized may elude a twenty-first-century American. When the apocryphal book of Judith opens with "it was the twelfth year of the reign of Nebuchadnezzar, who ruled over the Assyrians in the great city of Nineveh," most scholars believe that it makes errors so egregious that any ancient reader would have understood it as ironic rather than as a truly historical preface, as any present-day reader would understand a story that began with "it happened at the time when Napoleon Bonaparte was king of

6. Dan Brown, *The Da Vinci Code* (New York: Doubleday, 2003), 2.

England, and Otto von Bismarck was on the throne of Mexico."[7] The outlandish episodes found throughout the book of Jonah similarly lead most scholars to classify it not as history, biography, or prophecy but as a parody or a satire. To read the book of Revelation as a list of specific, if veiled, prophecies of events far in the future instead of reading it as a specimen of apocalyptic literature situated in its own time is likewise to risk misunderstanding its bizarre symbols, which may have functioned like the donkeys and elephants one finds today in political cartoons. Biblical authors rarely specify the genre in which they are writing because, however opaque their works may seem to contemporary readers, they could usually depend on their original audience to get it.

Letters are among the literary genres from antiquity that are still used today. For this reason, their literary form does not present the same interpretive challenges as some other genres. But modern literary genres are not identical to their ancient counterparts. Reading an ancient letter is similar to and yet different from reading a letter today. Letter-writing conventions have changed over time, sometimes quite radically. In some ways, the changes that have taken place over the last decade or so with the emergence of new communications technologies have affected the role of letters in society more than over the preceding century. Writers in antiquity, who frequently comment that speaking face to face is the ideal way to communicate and maintain relationships, resort to letters only out of necessity. According to a recent poll, by contrast, only 53 percent of teenagers say that their favorite way to communicate with their friends is "in person." Cell phones, instant messaging, email, and text messages are the preferred communication methods for more than one-third of teenagers.[8] Conspicuously absent from this list is the letter. Each new medium, while similar to the letter, has its own distinct conventions and typical uses. An email message, for example, is not simply a letter in electronic form. The role of email, moreover, has evolved substantially in its still short history, with many viewing it "as something you use to

7. C. C. Torrey, *The Apocryphal Literature: A Brief Introduction* (New Haven: Yale University Press, 1945), 89.

8. Dana Markow, "Friendships in the Age of Social Networking Websites," *Harris Interactive Trends and Tudes* 5.9 (October 2006): 1–5.

talk to 'old people,' institutions, or to send complex instructions to large groups."[9]

This volume focuses on the literary genre of the letter in ancient Greece and Rome. Who wrote letters? Who read them? What did a letter look like? What types of letters were in use? What topics were discussed in letters? Comparison and contrast with modern letters reveal the distinctive conventions, forms, and purposes of ancient letters like those of Paul.

Paul and His Letters

If the birth and growth of Christianity is the most significant, far-reaching cultural development of the last two thousand years, and if the spread of Christianity is intimately related to the influence of the New Testament, then it is perhaps no hyperbole to name Paul, who wrote a substantial portion of the New Testament, the most significant writer in the history of Western civilization. Friends and enemies of Paul—there are many members of each camp—can largely agree on his historical significance even as they disagree on whether his legacy is a cause for celebration or mourning. He is a controversial figure today, as he was also in his own time. Once a persecutor of Christians, he becomes the new faith's most zealous and successful missionary.

As intriguing as his biography may be, Paul's life has had less influence than his thought. The earliest sources for discovering Paul's thought are his own letters and the Acts of the Apostles. Because Acts is a third-person narrative by another author, the letters provide the most direct contact with Paul's own thinking. How should one go about studying the letters? Scholars take three different approaches.

First, a chronological or historical approach has as its aim the description of Paul's thought as it develops over time. This approach is common when the focus is on various tensions found in his writings. How does one explain, for example, the different attitudes toward

---

9. Amanda Lenhart and Mary Madden, "Social Networking Websites and Teens," Pew Research Center: Internet and Technology, January 7, 2007, www.pewresearch.org/internet/2007/01/07/social-networking-websites-and-teens (accessed September 20, 2009).

marriage in 1 Corinthians and Ephesians? Changes in Paul's thought over time sometimes account for the differences.

To study Paul's letters in this way, it is necessary to know when they were written. And that is precisely the problem with this approach. Dating Paul's letters is notoriously difficult. Like most writings from antiquity, they lack copyright dates. They often include little more than circumstantial evidence and vague details to enable historians to assign a date to them. It is impossible to establish an absolute chronology, that is, to place the letters accurately in precise years on a calendar. A relative chronology that simply places the letters in the proper order of composition is more feasible but not without considerable challenges. There is widespread disagreement on how to date the letters. Solving the problem is not as simple as consulting the experts—the experts themselves do not all agree (see appendix 1).

In principle, of course, it would be immensely beneficial to know exactly when and in what order Paul wrote his letters. Every bit of available information furnishes a piece to the historical puzzle, if only one knows where to put it. But in practice it can be risky to link an interpretation of a letter too closely to a precise dating or even to its specific placement in the sequence of Pauline letters. Riskier still are attempts to sketch a comprehensive picture of Paul's thinking as it develops over time in this manner. If one date or the order is incorrect, it can all come tumbling down like a house of cards. This is true above all for the disputed letters, those that many scholars believe were not written by Paul, but for the undisputed letters as well.[10] The trick is to take advantage of all the relevant facts that are known with relative certainty without pinning everything on a particular, speculative reconstruction of the world behind the text. The letters are sufficiently rich in content that one need not make reading Paul revolve around chronology.

10. Calvin J. Roetzel mentions two such examples in *Paul: The Man and the Myth* (Columbia: University of South Carolina Press, 1998), 179: (1) It makes a significant difference if Galatians is later than Romans. Most scholars assume that Galatians is earlier, and that his views in that letter have time to circulate and provoke a reaction, which requires the theological response seen in Romans. (2) Earlier in his career, did Paul have an intense expectation of Jesus's imminent second coming that "relaxed" over time? If 1 Thessalonians is not relatively early, it is difficult to find support for this view in his letters.

Who Wrote Paul's Letters?

Thirteen letters in the New Testament bear Paul's name. Doubts about their authorship were rare before the nineteenth century, but scholars have questioned the authorship of several of the letters over the past few centuries. Today, it is widely, though not universally, agreed that seven letters were definitely written by Paul (the undisputed letters) and six were likely written by someone else (the disputed letters):

Undisputed Letters	Disputed Letters
Romans	Ephesians
1 Corinthians	Colossians
2 Corinthians	2 Thessalonians
Galatians	1 Timothy
Philippians	2 Timothy
1 Thessalonians	Titus
Philemon	

Debate about these disputes is the subject of chapter 6. Most of the references in this volume will be to passages in undisputed letters. Reference to the disputed letters will also be made because, either by comparison or contrast, they illustrate something about the literary genre in which Paul is composing, whether or not Paul is their author.

Second, a theological or thematic approach attempts to elucidate particular ideas or themes found in the letters or an overarching theological system present throughout Paul's body of work as a whole. What does Paul believe about God, Jesus, salvation, history, the Jews, the Roman state, human nature, freedom, redemption, sin, Satan, prayer, sex, the Holy Spirit, righteousness, slavery, and baptism? And how do these concepts fit together in a coherent system?

The difficulties with this approach are that Paul's thoughts on a given topic are not always clear and that the fit between various concepts is not always self-evident. Sources for reconstructing his thought are limited, consisting chiefly of the thirteen letters in the New Testament bearing his name. Of these thirteen, are some more valuable than others? Have some of them been written by someone else using "Paul" as a pseudonym? How does one distinguish ideas that are central to Paul's thinking from those that are peripheral? It is not as simple as determining to focus on the real Paul since this requires some prior sense of what is real and what is not, which is in turn based on the same letters the interpreter is seeking to understand.

One might attempt to understand Paul according to the standard categories employed in systematic theology, such as creation, revelation, ethics, justification, eschatology, sanctification, and the church. A flaw in this approach is its assumption that Paul is writing systematic theology. He is not. His writings undeniably contain material that is theological in nature. But he is writing letters, not treatises or formal essays like those of Thomas Aquinas or Karl Barth. To read Paul's letters as if they were theological essays is to expect a level of precision, organization, and comprehensiveness that he likely did not intend to meet. Presenting Paul's thoughts in forms and categories not of his choosing does not always distort them, yet it increases the likelihood of distortion by pulling them out of their original context.

Third, an epistolary approach acknowledges that Paul's thoughts are not directly available. Only the form in which he communicated his thoughts to various audiences survives. Paul wrote letters. A letter is not a transparent vehicle for delivering ideas. The epistolary genre itself contributes to the shape those ideas take. Marshall McLuhan's famous phrase "the medium is the message" may be a slight overstatement, but there is no doubt that the medium by which content is delivered affects an individual's understanding of that content. It also affects the content itself. If a writer wants to make a point in the form of a movie, for instance, it generally cannot exceed two hours in length or it will exhaust the attention span of the audience. Serious discussion of politics or philosophy is best conducted in some forum other than the Twitter website, which limits comments to a mere 140 characters.

Like other genres, letters possess distinctive capacities and limitations. In his letters, Paul is frequently trying to make a theological point or encourage certain types of moral behavior. An essay might be a more suitable form for theological exposition, but it lacks the letter's personal touch, which is often more effective in persuading a reader than is pure reason. Stories have more power than letters to shape moral character, but they are more prone to misconstruing than letters, where an author like Paul can say exactly what he expects of his audience. In order to agree or disagree with Paul's theology or his ethics, it is necessary to have an accurate understanding of his theology and ethics, which is in turn contingent upon a proper discernment of the genre in which he is writing.

Serious study of Paul specifically as a letter writer began only in the last century or so, spurred in part by the discovery of hundreds of ancient letters in places like Egypt, where the climate prevented their decay. Comparing Paul's writings to these everyday letters, Adolf Deissmann made a distinction between the "letter" and the more formal literary "epistle." Paul was writing for his contemporaries, not for public consumption or with an eye for posterity. "Almost all the mistakes that have ever been made in the study of St. Paul's life and work," he asserts, "have arisen from neglect of the fact that his writings are non-literary and letter-like in character."[11] All too often, he continues, study of Paul begins with Romans, the first letter to appear in the New Testament table of contents but the least typical of his writings, when it ought to begin with Philemon, the last to appear but the most letter-like in form.

Although Deissmann may have exaggerated the situation—subsequent decades have decisively shown that scholars are perfectly able to make all sorts of mistakes about Paul even when they recognize that he is writing letters—his analysis serves as a reminder that reading Paul is an exercise in reading other people's mail. Romans, 1–2 Corinthians, Galatians, and all the rest were written and sent to Romans, Corinthians, and Galatians. They are examples of occasional literature; that is, they were composed for a particular occasion. Paul articulates his thoughts in response to a specific situation. Had he confronted a different situation, his response might have taken a different shape. He is not like a college professor who writes a book out of intellectual curiosity or because of the professional demand to "publish or perish." The letters have a dialogical

11. Adolf Deissmann, *Light from the Ancient East: The New Testament Illustrated by Recently Discovered Texts of the Graeco-Roman World*, trans. Lionel R. M. Strachan, 4th ed. (New York: Doran, 1927), 234.

character. They provide a snapshot of a conversation in process, with reference to things that have been said earlier ("by word of mouth or by letter"; 2 Thess. 2:15) and to things that will be discussed later (1 Cor. 11:34).

This is not to say that he is simply making it up as he goes or that his thinking is constantly in flux. Rather, it is a caution against reading the letters as if they were comprehensive formulations of his theology. Some scholars are wary even of attempting to summarize Paul's thought by coordinating his statements from separate letters, since his ideas about love or the resurrection as they are found in Philippians and 1 Corinthians may ultimately be irreconcilable, and scholars could warp Paul's ideas by trying to reconcile them within a system. This aversion to reading the letters synoptically is perhaps overcautious, but at the same time it is prudent to carry out comparisons between letters only after one has a firm grasp of how Paul uses a term or concept (e.g., faith, righteousness, flesh) in a single letter.

The following chapters provide an overview of subjects, strategies, and concerns of immediate relevance for anyone who wishes to read Paul's letters. Chapter 1 takes stock of the ways in which Paul participates in the culture and society of the first-century Mediterranean inhabited by other Jews, Greeks, and Romans. Chapter 2 surveys the range of letter genres and subgenres available to Paul and considers possible classifications for each of the letters. Chapter 3 discusses the rhetoric and formal structure of the letters alongside those of Paul's contemporaries and examines the extent to which the form of his arguments influences their function and content. Chapter 4 demonstrates how paying attention to the original audiences of the letters gives the reader sharper insights into what Paul was trying to accomplish. Chapter 5 highlights how Paul's habits as a reader of the Old Testament influence what he writes. Chapter 6 looks at debates about the authorship of the letters and the senses in which it affects how one approaches them. The epilogue looks briefly at letters in early Christianity that Paul did not write. Each chapter concludes with a short list of discussion questions and with a select bibliography for those who want to pursue a topic further than space permits here.

For Further Discussion

1. What does it mean to read the Bible "just like any other text"?
2. Do questions about the literary genre of Paul's letters belong to "the world behind the text," "the world of the text," or "the world in front of the text"?
3. What are the pitfalls of reading Paul's letters without taking their literary genre into account?

For Further Reading

Achtemeier, Paul J. "Some Things in Them Hard to Understand: Reflections on an Approach to Paul." *Interpretation* 38 (1984): 254–67.

Barrett, C. K. *Paul: An Introduction to His Thought*. Louisville: Westminster John Knox, 1994.

Cousar, Charles B. *The Letters of Paul*. Interpreting Biblical Texts. Nashville: Abingdon, 1996.

Decker, W. M. *Epistolary Practices: Letter Writing in America before Telecommunications*. Chapel Hill: University of North Carolina Press, 1998.

Fitzmyer, Joseph A. *Paul and His Theology: A Brief Sketch*. 2nd ed. Englewood Cliffs, NJ: Prentice Hall, 1989.

Gorman, Michael J. *Apostle of the Crucified Lord: A Theological Introduction to Paul and His Letters*. Grand Rapids: Eerdmans, 2004.

Harlow, Alvin F. *Old Post Bags: The Story of the Sending of a Letter in Ancient and Modern Times*. New York: Appleton, 1928.

Hengel, Martin, and Anna Maria Schwemer. *Paul between Damascus and Antioch: The Unknown Years*. Translated by John M. Bowden. Louisville: Westminster John Knox, 1997.

Hooker, Morna D. *Paul: A Short Introduction*. Oxford: OneWorld, 2003.

Horrell, David G. *An Introduction to the Study of Paul*. 2nd ed. London: T&T Clark, 2006.

Keck, Leander E. *Paul and His Letters*. 2nd ed. Philadelphia: Fortress, 1988.

Klauck, Hans-Josef. *Ancient Letters and the New Testament: A Guide to Context and Exegesis*. Waco: Baylor University Press, 2006.

McKenzie, Steven L. *How to Read the Bible*. Oxford: Oxford University Press, 2005.

Meeks, Wayne A., and John T. Fitzgerald, eds. *The Writings of Saint Paul*. 2nd ed. New York: Norton, 2007.

Murphy-O'Connor, Jerome. *Paul: A Critical Life*. Oxford: Oxford University Press, 1996.

————. *Paul the Letter-Writer: His World, His Options, His Skills*. Collegeville, MN: Michael Glazier/Liturgical Press, 1995.

Roetzel, Calvin J. *Paul: The Man and the Myth*. Studies on Personalities of the New Testament. Minneapolis: Fortress, 1999.

Ruden, Sarah. *Paul among the People: The Apostle Reinterpreted and Reimagined in His Own Time*. New York: Pantheon, 2010.

Schnelle, Udo. *Apostle Paul: His Life and Theology*. Translated by M. Eugene Boring. Grand Rapids: Baker Academic, 2003.

Schreiner, Thomas R. *Interpreting the Pauline Epistles*. 2nd ed. Grand Rapids: Baker Academic, 2011.

1

Paul's Cultural Contexts

Viewing a picture is not entirely unlike interpreting one of the letters Paul is frequently depicted writing in paintings from the Renaissance to the present. A picture, so the saying goes, is worth a thousand words. Consider this picture: A man with brown skin in evident distress pounds on one side of a window. On the other side sits a figure with horns, a tail, and cloven hooves, calmly whistling as he peruses an album cover bearing the title "New Age Music's Greatest Hits," the turntable in front of him apparently broadcasting the music through the large speakers on the other side of the glass. Below the picture appears the caption "Charlie Parker's private hell."

Gary Larson published this comic strip as part of his popular *Far Side* series in 1990. It is supposed to be funny. And funny it is, provided that one is familiar with the general cultural context and catches the specific allusions it contains. What knowledge is needed to get the joke? Larson assumes that his readers will know who Charlie Parker is—that he was a legendary jazz saxophonist—what "new age" signifies, what the devil looks like, what records are, and that hell is supposed to be unpleasant. All this information, and much more, is encoded in this one panel. Another approach to interpreting this comic strip is to ask what it reveals about Larson and his late twentieth-century milieu. For starters, it is apparent that new age music is widely despised—at least by those who know and love the music of Charlie Parker—since Larson can make fun of it and count on a laugh. Accordingly, new age music fits perfectly with a depiction of hell, but only if the devil specifically tailors the punishment to the individual, a notion familiar to most people, whether or not they have read Dante. Further information may be gleaned from other details: Turntables are still in use. The image of the devil is instantly recognizable. Other features raise as many questions as they answer: Does Larson believe in hell? Does he think that his audience believes in hell? Most Americans tell pollsters they do, but is their willingness to joke about something so grave as eternal torment an indicator that belief in hell is wide but not very deep?

If a single picture with a four-word caption implies, evokes, relates to, suggests, presupposes, and hints at so many different social, cultural, historical, and religious concerns, how much more so do larger and more complex artifacts like Paul's letters to the Romans or the Philippians? To read and understand Paul's letters, it is absolutely necessary to know something about the wider world in which he lived and wrote. The death of Jesus, according to Paul, marks a decisive intervention into human history by the God of Israel. "Christ crucified," however, is "a stumbling block to Jews and foolishness to Gentiles" (1 Cor. 1:23). That Christianity spread as quickly as it did is surprising given that its central message struck a discordant note with every conceivable demographic—the categories "Jew" and "gentile," after all, cover all of humanity. Christianity begins with the execution of a Jewish teacher, but it is also important to remember that he was killed by Roman authorities and that the earliest writings of the fledgling sect survive only in Greek. From the outset, then, the Christian movement cut across ordinary ethnic, cultural, social, and linguistic boundaries.

Sometimes the encounter between the Jews who were Jesus's first followers and the Greco-Roman world is quite explicit, as when Paul reminds the centurion about to flog him that he has certain legal rights as a Roman citizen (Acts 22:25–29), or when he urges the Roman Christians to obey the emperor and pay their taxes (Rom. 13:1–7). Elsewhere in his letters the influence of Greek and Roman culture is less conspicuous but no less profound. Attempting to articulate the new faith, Paul and his readers are engaged in the process of creating a distinctively Christian identity. But it was not creation *ex nihilo*. Although novel claims about Jesus function as a common denominator, Christian identity is formed from preexisting elements in the cultural contexts of those who had converted, Jew and gentile alike.

It would be impossible to provide anything like a comprehensive overview of the world Paul inhabited in an entire book, much less in a single chapter. This chapter will survey a small selection of concepts, images, and motifs from the Greco-Roman milieu in which Christianity emerged and will illustrate their significance for understanding Paul's letters. Additional resources may be found in the bibliography at the end of the chapter.

Paul among Greeks and Romans

By virtue of his living at the same time and in the same culture as his neighbors who do not believe that Jesus is the Messiah, Paul takes for granted any number of the same things about the way the world operates. Although the real world as experienced by real people is not easily organized into separate compartments, for the sake of convenience it is helpful to observe Paul's background under a handful of distinct headings.

Judaism and Hellenism

Paul was a Jew. To appreciate this aspect of Paul's background, an acquaintance with the Hebrew Bible is essential, but it is only a beginning. Just as there is much more to understanding English history than kings and queens and the Magna Carta, understanding Judaism in the first century involves much more than reading its officially sanctioned Scriptures. Jewish life and thought continued to thrive during the so-called intertestamental period between the time of Nehemiah and the last of the biblical prophets (ca. 400 BCE) and the birth of Jesus. Even though they were never a part of anyone's canon of Scripture, writings such as *Testaments of the Twelve*

Key Events Shaping Paul's World	
586 BCE	The Babylonians destroy the temple in Jerusalem, sending most of the Jews into exile.
538 BCE	After the Persians defeat the Babylonians, Cyrus the Great issues a proclamation permitting the exiled Judeans to return to Jerusalem and rebuild the temple.
333 BCE	Alexander the Great conquers the Persians and establishes Greek-Macedonian rule over Palestine.
167–164 BCE	The Maccabees in Jerusalem stage a revolt against the Seleucid Greeks in response to the program of forced hellenization conducted by Antiochus IV.
63 BCE	Under Pompey, Rome begins its occupation of Palestine.
31 BCE	Octavian (later Augustus Caesar) defeats Antony and Cleopatra at the Battle of Actium. Four years later, he assumes the powers of an emperor, and Rome officially becomes an empire.
70 CE	Rome destroys the Second Temple in putting down the Jewish revolt that had begun a few years earlier.

Patriarchs, 1–2 Enoch, Apocalypse of Abraham, and *Ascension of Isaiah* attest to the rich diversity of Jewish literature in the centuries preceding Paul's appearance on the scene.[1]

Jewish diversity in the first century was not limited to the literary sphere. Judaism was every bit as diverse when it came to politics and theology. Institutions and ideas such as land, covenant, law, and temple were recognized by Jews of all stripes, albeit with differing emphases and interpretations of their meaning. First-century Palestine was home to four main sects of Judaism. These sects were somewhat analogous to Christian denominations today, though the majority of Jews were not official members of any sect. Pharisaic Judaism placed special emphasis on the interpretation and adaptation of Mosaic law to all areas of life. The Sadducees were closely associated with activities at the temple in Jerusalem—the high priest was typically drawn from their ranks—and were seen by many Jews as overly friendly with the Roman overlords. The Essenes, who comprised an austere community

1. These and dozens of other Jewish writings from the Second Temple period are available in English translation in *The Old Testament Pseudepigrapha*, ed. James H. Charlesworth, 2 vols. (New York: Doubleday, 1983–85).

based in the desert at Qumran near the Dead Sea, viewed all other groups as having deviated from the authentic faith of Israel. The Zealots aimed at throwing off the Roman yoke by military means. Within this field of play, Paul plants his flag with the Pharisees (Phil. 3:5; cf. Acts 23:6; 26:5), which probably explains his preoccupation with the role of the law in Romans, Galatians, and other letters. Of these four groups, only the Pharisees survived the Jewish revolt that ended with the destruction of the temple in 70 CE. The survival of so many of Paul's letters, relative to other early Christian writers, may be due to the relevance they had late in the first century when the Pharisees were the primary rivals opposing the Christians in their claim to represent fidelity to Torah.

Conditions were different in the Diaspora, a term used for the Jewish community located outside the land of Israel. Sizable populations of Jews across the Mediterranean, in cities like Paul's hometown of Tarsus, had put down roots centuries before the birth of Christianity. After the Babylonian destruction of the Jerusalem temple in 586 BCE, most Jews went into exile and their descendants never returned to the land. Jews in the Diaspora still outnumbered those in Palestine in the first century. Even in cities with large Jewish populations such as Rome and Alexandria, Jews were a minority everywhere in the Diaspora. Jews commanded the respect of their gentile neighbors for their strict moral code and the antiquity of their customs. At the same time, they were frequently the object of ridicule and prejudice on account of what many non-Jews saw as cultural insularity, bizarre dietary restrictions, loyalty to foreign interests, and the barbaric practice of circumcising male infants.[2] Little wonder that the message of justification apart from "works of the law" appealed to many gentiles, especially those like Titus who, according to Gal. 2:3, "was not compelled to be circumcised." (From Acts 16:3, it appears that Timothy was not so lucky.)

Always cognizant of their calling to be "a peculiar people" (Deut. 14:2 KJV) wherever they called home, for Diaspora Jews like Paul the temptation to assimilate was nevertheless ever present. Engagement with gentile culture was unavoidable, beginning in the fourth century

2. See Peter Schäfer, *Judeophobia: Attitudes toward the Jews in the Ancient World* (Cambridge, MA: Harvard University Press, 1997).

BCE, when Alexander the Great established Greek military control over much of the region and Greek became the common language of the Mediterranean basin. This fusion between Greek cultures and the peoples conquered by Alexander is called Hellenism. Without a male heir to succeed him at his death in 323 BCE, Alexander divided his empire between three of his top generals, leaving Palestine and Judea caught at a crossroads, with political and cultural traffic flowing in multiple directions.

After generations of life outside the homeland, for many Jews the decision was not whether to assimilate to Hellenistic culture, but in what way and to what extent. Ben Sira's grandson translated his wisdom writings into Greek and in his preface acknowledged that "what was originally expressed in Hebrew does not have exactly the same sense when translated into another language" and that even the Law and the Prophets "differ not a little when read in the original." His book was subsequently included in the Greek translation of the Hebrew Bible, called the Septuagint. Other Jewish writers did not have the same qualms. Ezekiel the Tragedian presented the story of the exodus in the form of a Greek drama. Philo of Alexandria synthesized Israelite religion with Pythagorean, Platonic, and Stoic philosophy. Josephus related a story about Aristotle meeting a Jew who "not only spoke Greek, but had the soul of a Greek" (*Against Apion* 1.179–81). While Paul did not go so far as Theodotus, who retold Gen. 34 in dactylic hexameter after the fashion of Homer, he felt no need to defend his use of the Septuagint when quoting the Jewish scriptures.

Paul conducted most of his ministry in the Diaspora but also had regular contact with Jerusalem and the Jewish Christian groups residing there. Jerusalem was not exempt from Hellenistic influence, nor were those who sought actively to escape it. The case of the Maccabean revolt against the Seleucid king Antiochus IV (167–164 BCE) provides a poignant illustration. Although the Maccabees succeeded in driving the pagans from Jerusalem after the desecration of the temple, they won the battle, so to speak, only to lose the war: the story of their struggle to resist the encroachment of Hellenistic culture has not survived in Hebrew but only in manuscripts translated into Greek. The Christian faith one encounters in Paul's letters, then, is born out of a Judaism that was immersed in Greek and Roman culture for centuries.

Roman Rule

Rome effectively dominates the Mediterranean from the second century onward, even if the Roman Republic does not give way to the Roman Empire until 27 BCE. Its impact on Jewish life was enormous but not uniform. Jewish responses to Roman rule, like later Christian responses, were accordingly mixed. A scene from the 1979 comedy *Life of Brian* nicely captures the ambivalence of Jews on the subject of empire. Plotting the overthrow of the Roman state, the leader of a band of Jewish revolutionaries asks, rhetorically, "What have the Romans ever done for us?" His fellow rebels, as it turns out, can think of several answers to that question: roads, aqueducts, sanitation, wine, medicine, education, irrigation, public order, and peace after nearly a century of civil war. Whatever drawbacks came with life as part of a subject people—and there were many, including heavy taxation, loss of political self-determination, slavery, and military occupation—it could not be denied that the *Pax Romana* also brought many benefits.[3] At the very least, many first-century Jews realized that the Roman Empire showed no signs of crumbling any time in the near future and, instead of quixotically resisting this political reality, they got along as best they could.

Rome's attitudes toward and treatment of the Jews were likewise uneven. In Paul's time, Christianity was still a sect within Judaism. The Roman authorities made little effort to sort out the esoteric internal disputes about the law and other matters that divided one type of Jew from another. Christians and Jews were largely indistinguishable from a Roman perspective until later in the first century. Although it did not occur as often as is widely thought, persecution of one frequently meant persecution of the other.

What motivated religious persecution in the first century? The earliest surviving references to Christianity made by Roman writers provide a clue. A common thread appears in the brief comments found in Suetonius, Tacitus, and Pliny, Roman historians writing early in the second century. Tacitus, in describing the fire at Rome during

---

3. Paul and other Christian missionaries take advantage of the extensive system of roads constructed by Rome in order to spread their message far and wide. Safe transportation also facilitated the regular postal service first established by Augustus Caesar, though Paul was not able to make use of it (Suetonius, *Augustus* 49).

Roman Emperors in the First Century	
27 BCE–14 CE	Augustus
14–37	Tiberius
37–41	Gaius (nicknamed Caligula)
41–54	Claudius
54–68	Nero
68–69	Galba
69	Otho
69	Vitellius
69–79	Vespasian
79–81	Titus
81–96	Domitian
96–98	Nerva
98–117	Trajan

Nero's reign, speaks of Christianity as a "pernicious superstition" breaking out after being temporarily checked by the death of Jesus (*Annales* 15.44). Recounting Nero's punishment of the Christians, whom the emperor blamed for the fire, Suetonius calls them "a class of men given over to a new and mischievous superstition" (*Nero* 16.2). According to early church tradition, Paul is executed in the aftermath of the fire. Pliny the Younger, in a letter to Trajan, similarly describes the Christians of Bithynia as adherents of "a degenerate superstition carried to extravagant lengths" (*Epistle* 10.96). "Superstition" (Greek *deisidaimonia*; Latin *superstitio*) is the standard category in first-century Mediterranean culture for denigrating "debased" religion. It includes a wide range of irrational beliefs and customs and old wives' tales. Especially in Roman sources, superstition is connected to foreign cults and, as a result, is often considered politically subversive (Cicero, *De divinatione* 2.72.148; Suetonius, *Claudius* 25.5). For this reason, many writers apply this label to the Jews as well (Cicero, *Pro Flacco* 67). Rome was generally quite tolerant of foreign religions so long as they posed no threat to public order. But their tolerance had its limits, as Jerusalem learned when Roman armies destroyed the temple in 70 CE in the course of quelling the Jewish revolt.

Greek and Roman Philosophy

"The subject that I am about to discuss is most philosophical, that is, whether devout reason is sovereign over the emotions." What sort of work would begin in this fashion? A philosophical treatise? A dramatic narrative? A funeral oration? A celebration of religious faith? All of these apply to 4 Maccabees, from which these lines are taken. The author tells the story of seven unnamed brothers, their mother, and the aged Eleazar, who undergo brutal persecution by Antiochus IV for their refusal to abandon their Jewish customs. Included in the Septuagint, 4 Maccabees inspired many Jews living in the Hellenistic period during which it was written. Curiously, however, the convictions of the author and of the characters would sound almost as natural coming from the mouth of a Stoic philosopher as from a Sadducee or Pharisee.

As the author of 4 Maccabees unwittingly illustrates, the distinction between religion and philosophy is not a terribly sharp one in the Hellenistic period. Few today would confuse religion with philosophy or use the terms interchangeably. Rightly or wrongly, the popular stereotype of the philosopher is one who is absorbed in abstract questions and out of touch with the everyday concerns of ordinary people. Philosophy is frequently associated with such terms as "navel gazing," "hair splitting," and "logic chopping." Before a large audience at the 1998 World Philosophy Congress, the leading thinkers of the day were asked, "What have we learned from philosophy in the twentieth century?" Their response was to argue about the definition of "we" and "learned." Another admitted, "I'm going to have to pass." During the Hellenistic period, such obtuseness is less common. Philosophers increasingly spurned abstract questions for more practical ones. This concern for how to live a happy, fulfilled life can be seen in the titles of essays written by Epictetus, who wrote "On Tranquility," "On Friendship," "Against a Person Who Had Once Been Detected in Adultery," "Against Those Who Wish to Be Admired," "On Exercise," and "On Finery in Dress," among others. Today one is more likely to encounter these topics in a sermon by a preacher than in an essay by a philosopher.

Along with the older schools of Plato and Aristotle, Stoicism and Epicureanism were the leading schools of philosophy in the Hellenistic world. The goal of Epicureanism was to attain *ataraxia*, or "freedom from disturbance." Stoicism saw harmful emotions like fear as the greatest threat to human flourishing and thus promised to help its adherents reach a state of *apatheia*, or "freedom from passion." Stoics like Seneca (4 BCE–65 CE) and Epictetus (ca. 55–130 CE) and Epicureans like Lucretius (ca. 94–55 BCE) and Philodemus (ca. 110–40 BCE) furiously criticized each other as well as many aspects of popular

> ### Letters Etched in Stone
>
> Devotees of famous philosophers often took the initiative to preserve and propagate the teachings of the master. None show greater zeal than Diogenes of Oenoanda, an Epicurean of the second century CE who lived in an area of Asia Minor traveled often by the apostle Paul. Diogenes set up a rectangular piazza and had inscribed on it his own treatises and letters about Epicurean teachings as well as a number of letters by Epicurus himself. Standing over two meters high, stretching for nearly eighty meters, and containing approximately 25,000 words, it is thought to be the largest inscription produced in the ancient world. Much of it still survives, and archaeologists continue to discover new portions of it on a regular basis.

religion. But they had in common a firm belief, shared also with Judaism and Christianity, that ideas have consequences, that what one thinks is indelibly tied to how one lives. Over against the popular syncretism promoted by Alexander wherein elements from disparate religions were freely mixed and matched, they insisted on rigorously examining systems of belief and behavior for coherence and consistency. Hellenistic philosophical schools were different in that they made exclusive claims on the loyalties of their adherents. They demanded what can accurately be termed a conversion experience, that is, a "reorientation of the soul of an individual, his deliberate turning from indifference or from an earlier form of piety to another, a turning which implies a consciousness that a great change is involved, that the old was wrong and the new is right."[4]

In this respect, too, they bore a family resemblance to fiercely monotheistic Jews and Christians like Paul, who informed the Galatians that anyone proclaiming a gospel contrary to the gospel he had proclaimed would be cursed (1:9).

Social Relations

Letters function as a medium for maintaining relationships previously established rather than creating relationships where they do not

---

4. Arthur Darby Nock, *Conversion: The Old and the New in Religion from Alexander the Great to Augustine of Hippo* (Oxford: Clarendon, 1933), 7.

Paul and Porphyry

The long-lasting literary culture shared by Paul and his pagan neighbors can be seen in the letter of the third-century Neoplatonic philosopher Porphyry to his wife Marcella. Both men are on a mission from God (cf. *Ad Marcellam* 4.58–59). Both write letters that combine philosophical and traditional religious teachings. Both write to encourage audiences distressed by the departure of their teachers (cf. 1 Thessalonians). Both recommend sexual continence (1 Cor. 7) and contend that the categories of male and female are of no importance (Gal. 3:28–29; *Ad Marcellam* 33.511–13). Both link faith, hope, and love as necessary for a godly life (1 Cor. 13:13; *Ad Marcellam* 24.376–78, though Porphyry uses *erōs* instead of *agapē* and adds "truth" to the other three virtues). Porphyry is well known as one of the most forceful critics of Christianity in late antiquity; thus the similarities with Paul are all the more noteworthy.

---

already exist. In the Greco-Roman world, the three most important relationships are those between (1) members of the same household/family, (2) friends, and (3) patrons and clients.[5]

The basic unit of Mediterranean society was the family. Many of the letters surviving from antiquity show family members conducting ordinary household affairs, like paying bills, reporting on the health of loved ones, and requesting favors. Some of the family business, however, may strike modern readers as not so ordinary, as when an Egyptian named Hilarion directs his pregnant wife Alis to take care of the child if it is a boy and to abandon it if it is a girl (Oxyrhynchus Papyrus 744). Adoption of adult males was also very common in ancient Greece and Rome, usually for the purpose of perpetuating the family name and ensuring the proper disposition of the father's estate. Several passages in Paul's letters reflect complex legal and social conventions, even as he uses the ideas of adoption and inheritance as metaphors (Rom. 8:12–25; 9:4; Gal. 4:1–7; Eph. 1:5). Another aspect of family life that is alien to Paul's present-day readers is the inclusion of slaves in the household. Paul's characterization of the Mosaic law in Gal. 3:23–26 makes much more sense when one knows that a

---

5. See Stanley K. Stowers, *Letter Writing in Greco-Roman Antiquity* (Philadelphia: Westminster, 1986), 27–31.

paidagōgos is a slave put in charge of a young boy at home and school until he reaches maturity.

Nowhere in Paul's letters does he use the words "friend" or "friendship."[6] To assume from this silence that Paul has no friends would be a mistake. Plato, Aristotle, Cicero, Epictetus, and other philosophers wrote at great length about friendship. While Latin *amicitia* tends to have more political connotations than Greek *philia*, there is plenty of common ground. Plutarch, a near contemporary of Paul, gives a good sense of the conventional wisdom in his essays "On Having Many Friends" and "How to Tell a Flatterer from a Friend." Friends have all things in common. A friend is a "second self." Quality trumps quantity because a multitude of friends inevitably divides one's loyalties and works against the intimate companionship that is the hallmark of true friendship. Only a chameleon could adapt itself to the bewildering number and variety of friends one often finds, say, in modern social-networking circles (Plutarch, *De amicorum multitudine* 96f–97b). When Paul exhorts the Philippians to stand firm "in one spirit, . . . with one mind" (Phil. 1:27; 2:2–5) or boasts of his frankness with the Corinthians (2 Cor. 1:17; 10:1–13:10) or describes the pain he feels at being apart from the Thessalonians (1 Thess. 2:17–3:10), he is hitting the same notes one hears when ancient authors sing the praises of friendship.

The patron-client system is the formal name for the web of hierarchical relationships that define social life in the first century. A patron is an individual in a position of superiority vis-à-vis another individual. Those in a subordinate position are clients. Everyone was someone's patron (except for the lowest slave) and also someone's client (except for the emperor). To their patrons, clients owed honor and respect, which entailed greeting the patron in the morning and offering assistance in his political or economic endeavors. Patrons, in turn, used their power and influence to protect the client's interests, for example, by inviting them to parties or loaning them money. Paul calls Phoebe his patron (Rom. 16:1–2). As hosts of Paul and of church gatherings, Philemon, Stephanas, and Gaius (1 Cor. 16:15–18; Rom. 16:23) likewise acted as patrons, but the apostle's role in their

6. The NRSV is misleading on this point. It frequently renders the Greek word for "brother" (*adelphos*) into English as "friend."

conversions (1 Cor. 1:14–16; Philem. 19) put them in his debt, and so their relationship was not so straightforward. Dealings with Timothy, Titus, Priscilla, Peter, Apollos, and others mentioned in the letters also take place against this background, sometimes in accordance with and sometimes radically challenging the unspoken rules of the patron-client system.

Conclusion

Virtually every line of Paul's letters comes to life more vividly when viewed in the light of the broader cultural background. Admonitions to "extend hospitality" (Rom. 12:13; 1 Tim. 5:10; Titus 1:8) serve as a reminder that the options for missionaries and other travelers in need of lodging were limited to the private homes of acquaintances or rat-infested inns frequented by thieves and often doubling as brothels. Hairstyles in vogue among women in ancient Greece inform Paul's instructions regarding the behavior of prophets in 1 Cor. 11:2–16. Paul's assertion that the "citizenship" of the Philippians is "in heaven" (Phil. 3:20) is a subtle nod toward the city's status as a Roman colony. The likelihood that Roman slaves might receive their freedom—much greater than for their antebellum American counterparts—is surely relevant to the Corinthian slaves whom Paul tells, "Let each of you remain in the condition in which you were called" (1 Cor. 7:20–24). Examples like this could be multiplied ad infinitum.

These and many similar things simply go without saying, not only for Paul and his fellow Christians, but also for the Jews and gentiles who regard certain of his ideas about God and the world as exceedingly peculiar, if not downright blasphemous. Because so much of this common background remains unstated, it is possible to get the impression that Paul's teachings are even more unusual than they actually are. This is especially true of his engagement with Jewish opponents. Paul does not bother to rehash all the things on which they agree. Rather, he spends most of his energy on the points where they disagree. It is undeniable that Paul diverges from most Jews in his estimation of Jesus's significance. But the letters, with their narrow focus on the differences, inadvertently produce a skewed picture by making the conflict between the participants seem to be more acrimonious than is probably the case, sometimes giving rise to the unfortunate charge that Paul the Jew is anti-Jewish or anti-Semitic. Much of what Paul says in his letters is well within the normal bounds of intra-Jewish theological debates in the first century.

While it is unwise to read Paul's letters without paying adequate attention to the cultural context in which he is writing, it is also possible to read too much into the similarities and points of contact between Paul and his contemporaries. For a bit of perspective, consider the stunning number of parallels between the lives of Abraham Lincoln and John F. Kennedy. Lincoln and Kennedy were both elected to Congress in '46 and to the White House in '60. Both were the second-born sons in their families and had a sister die before becoming president. Both married twenty-four-year-old brunettes who spoke fluent French and had a child die while in office. John Wilkes Booth shot Lincoln from inside a theater and then fled to a warehouse, while Lee Harvey Oswald shot Kennedy from inside a warehouse and then fled to a theater. Lincoln was shot inside Ford's Theatre, and Kennedy was shot while riding in a Lincoln Continental, made by the Ford Motor Company. Both Booth and Oswald escaped and were killed before going to trial by bullets fired from a Colt revolver. Lincoln and Kennedy were both succeeded by Johnsons, former senators from Southern states who chose not to stand for reelection in '68.

The parallels between Lincoln and Kennedy are truly astonishing, and what they prove is . . . absolutely nothing. As impressive as they may surely seem, the similarities are no more than a coincidence. Even if they amounted to evidence of an elaborate conspiracy of cosmic proportions connecting Lincoln and Kennedy, it is hardly clear what such a conspiracy might mean. Noting the similarities between two items is not the same thing as explaining the relative significance of the similarities.

"Parallelomania" is a term coined to refer to the overly enthusiastic amassing of parallels between two figures or movements with insufficient regard for context, as if the parallels speak for themselves and demonstrate some substantive connection of profound significance.[7]

7. Samuel Sandmel, "Parallelomania," *Journal of Biblical Literature* 81 (1962): 1–13. Gian Biagio Conte prefers the term "comparisonitis," which he defines as "comparison for the sake of comparison" (*The Rhetoric of Imitation: Genre and Poetic*

Patterns of parallels are more instructive than isolated, arbitrarily selected terms or phrases. Differences, moreover, can reveal even more important clues about the relationship between various texts and traditions. Yes, Paul uses the same Greek word for "contentment" (*autarkeia*) as Stoic and Cynic philosophers who trumpet the virtue of self-sufficiency (2 Cor. 9:8; Phil. 4:11; 1 Tim. 6:6; cf. Epictetus, *Diatribai* 1.6.14), but they differ in the emphasis they put on it, in the importance they attach to it, in the methods they prescribe for attaining it, and in the way they see it complementing other virtues. Yes, Paul echoes themes similar to those found in Platonic and Stoic texts (that he may or may not have read) pertaining to the permissibility of taking one's own life, but that does not necessarily mean that he is contemplating suicide in Phil. 1:21–26.[8] To be sure, Paul strives to be "all things to all people" (1 Cor. 9:22), yet this notion, too, must be understood in its Greco-Roman context. Is he claiming to be like Proteus, the Greek god capable of assuming different shapes as the situation demands? Or is he highlighting the flexibility of his missionary and pedagogical strategy, as did Hellenistic philosophers such as Maximus of Tyre in his second-century treatise entitled "That a Philosopher's Discourse Is Adapted to Every Subject"? Some allusions and associations are more relevant than others in the complicated matrix of Mediterranean society. Taking stock of the ways in which Paul unthinkingly assumes, naturally conforms to, consciously departs from, creatively transforms, or suggests variations on the customs, conceptions, and conventions of his time and place is part and parcel of a close and careful reading of his letters.

·············· **For Further Discussion** ··············

1. How was Paul affected by the omnipresent reality of Roman rule? Is this influence explicit in his letters or only implicit?

Memory in Virgil and Other Latin Poets, trans. C. Segal [Ithaca: Cornell University Press, 1986], 23).

8. Even less likely is the theory, proposed by Arthur J. Droge, that Paul not only contemplated but actually committed suicide ("Did Paul Commit Suicide?" *Bible Review* 5 [December 1989]: 14–21).

2. What impact did Alexander the Great have on the world in which Paul wrote his letters?

3. During the Hellenistic and Roman periods, are religion and philosophy two species of the same genus, or are they fundamentally different types of pursuits? How does Paul orient himself with respect to the philosophers of his day?

4. To what extent, if any, is it appropriate to think of Paul's letters as a form of first-century Jewish literature?

For Further Reading

Barclay, J. M. G. *Jews in the Mediterranean Diaspora: From Alexander to Trajan (323 BCE–117 CE)*. Edinburgh: T&T Clark, 1996.

Barrett, C. K., ed. *The New Testament Background: Selected Documents*. Rev. ed. San Francisco: Harper, 1989.

Benko, S., and J. J. O'Rourke. *The Catacombs and the Colosseum: The Roman Empire as the Setting of Primitive Christianity*. Valley Forge, PA: Judson, 1971.

Burkert, Walter. *Greek Religion*. Translated by John Raffan. Cambridge, MA: Harvard University Press, 1985.

Cohen, S. J. D. *From the Maccabees to the Mishnah*. 2nd ed. Louisville: Westminster John Knox, 2006.

Collins, John J. *Between Athens and Jerusalem: Jewish Identity in the Hellenistic Diaspora*. New York: Crossroad, 1983.

Collins, Raymond F. *The Power of Images in Paul*. Collegeville, MN: Michael Glazier/Liturgical Press, 2008.

Dixon, Suzanne. *The Roman Family*. Baltimore: Johns Hopkins University Press, 1992.

Elliott, Neil, and Mark Reasoner. *Documents and Images for the Study of Paul*. Minneapolis: Fortress, 2010.

Engberg-Pedersen, Troels, ed. *Paul in His Hellenistic Context*. Minneapolis: Fortress, 1995.

Evans, Craig A. "Paul and the Pagans." In *Paul: Jew, Greek, and Roman*, edited by Stanley E. Porter, 117–39. Leiden: Brill, 2008.

Feldman, Louis H., and Meyer Reinhold, eds. *Jewish Life and Thought among Greeks and Romans: Primary Readings*. Philadelphia: Fortress, 1996.

Ferguson, Everett. *Backgrounds of Early Christianity*. 2nd ed. Grand Rapids: Eerdmans, 1993.

Finegan, Jack. *Myth and Mystery: An Introduction to the Pagan Religions of the Biblical World*. Grand Rapids: Baker, 1989.

Lefkowitz, Mary R., and Maureen B. Fant, eds. *Women's Life in Ancient Greece and Rome*. London: Duckworth, 1982.

Long, A. A. *Hellenistic Philosophy*. London: Duckworth, 1986.

MacMullen, Ramsay. *Enemies of the Roman Order*. Cambridge, MA: Harvard University Press, 1966.

Malherbe, Abraham J. *Social Aspects of Early Christianity*. Philadelphia: Fortress, 1983.

Martin, Luther. *Hellenistic Religions: An Introduction*. New York: Oxford University Press, 1987.

Meeks, Wayne A. *The First Urban Christians: The Social World of the Apostle Paul*. New Haven: Yale University Press, 1983.

Neusner, Jacob. *From Politics to Piety: The Emergence of Pharisaic Judaism*. Englewood Cliffs, NJ: Prentice-Hall, 1973.

Osiek, Carolyn, and David L. Balch. *Families in the New Testament World: Households and House Churches*. Louisville: Westminster John Knox, 1997.

Sampley, J. Paul, ed. *Paul in the Greco-Roman World: A Handbook*. Harrisburg, PA: Trinity, 2003.

Schiffman, Lawrence H., ed. *Texts and Traditions: A Source Reader for the Study of Second Temple and Rabbinic Judaism*. Hoboken, NJ: Ktav, 1997.

Segal, A. F. *Rebecca's Children: Judaism and Christianity in the Roman World*. Cambridge, MA: Harvard University Press, 1986.

Walbank, F. W. *The Hellenistic World*. Cambridge, MA: Harvard University Press, 1982.

Wiedemann, Thomas. *Greek and Roman Slavery*. Baltimore: Johns Hopkins University Press, 1981.

Wilken, Robert L. *The Christians as the Romans Saw Them*. New Haven: Yale University Press, 1984.

2

Letter Genres

Sherlock Holmes, Hercule Poirot, Miss Jane Marple, Perry Mason, Nancy Drew, Sam Spade, Encyclopedia Brown—sleuths of various stripes are among the most popular characters in print and on screen. Their appeal is only partly due to their quirky character traits. The mystery genre itself is what attracts large audiences. Readers know what to expect when they pick up a whodunit. Or, they know what *not* to expect. Ronald Knox spells out these expectations in his tongue-in-cheek "Ten Commandments of Detective Fiction."[1] Rather than presuming to lay down laws that did not already exist, he is simply articulating the rules of the genre that readers take for granted. When writers break these rules—for example, "The detective must not himself commit the crime," and "Twin brothers, and doubles generally, must not appear unless we have been duly prepared for them"—readers are sure to notice.

Every genre has its rules, and most writers break a rule now and then. The rules help readers know how to navigate a text. They define the medium through which the writer communicates. Departures from the norm send signals to the reader about what is distinctive or exceptional, and, for that reason, they merit close attention.

1. Ronald A. Knox, "Introduction," in *The Best English Detective Stories of 1928*, ed. R. A. Knox and H. Harrington (London: Faber & Faber, 1929), xi–xiv.

Reading Paul's letters begins with an awareness of their genre. They are letters, of course. But this recognition is only a beginning. Today letters fall into a wide range of categories: friendly letters, invitations, love letters, hate mail, letters of recommendation, résumé cover letters, thank you notes, letters to the editor, resignation letters, termination letters, condolence cards, donation letters, ransom notes, suicide notes, postcards, and so on. The range of categories in Greco-Roman antiquity is, if anything, even wider. Although reports of the death of the letter genre in the twenty-first century have been greatly exaggerated, anecdotal evidence and sales figures from the US Postal Service strongly suggest that letter writing is a waning custom. Letters played a larger role in literate society in the first century. Instruction in writing letters formed a part of the curriculum in schools attended by children of aristocrats and those who would go on to careers in a government bureaucracy. Secretaries, some of whom were slaves, also required basic training to perform their jobs. A number of epistolary handbooks were produced to meet this need and will be discussed in the following section. Letters even played a role in nonliterate society, where it was not uncommon to hire a scribe to draft correspondence for personal and official business.

Familiarity with the types of letters in general use among first-century writers is helpful because it makes it possible to see where Paul is following the rules and where he is breaking them. By identifying the genres he uses, modern readers have a clearer idea of what Paul is (or is not) trying to say and do by means of the letter. The original recipients of Paul's letters, too, would have known what to expect on the basis of the genre in which he wrote. The sender of a get-well-soon card or a birthday card, for example, has to do little more than sign his name to send the desired message. The card itself says it all. Where Paul follows epistolary convention, he is letting the genre do the work for him; where he deviates—even when he does not call attention to it—he does so for a reason.

Letter Genres in Ancient Greece and Rome

"Letter" and "epistle" are synonyms in English, though the latter strikes the ear as more formal or official. Adolf Deissmann, a pioneer in the modern study of Paul's letters, made a distinction between letters and epistles when he compared more refined writings like those of Plutarch and Epicurus with the hoards of papyrus documents discovered in Egyptian garbage dumps beginning late in the nineteenth century near the town of Oxyrhynchus. Epistles, according to Deissmann, are highly stylized works of art more or less parading as letters, while letters are genuinely private and personal, affording the reader a glimpse of everyday life. He classifies Paul's authentic letters as true letters. James, 1–2 Peter, and Jude, however, he classifies as epistles.[2]

Although Deissmann's categories are overly simplistic, the notion that it is important to classify letters according to type is not just a bias of modern scholars. Nor are readers the only ones who need to know about letter genres. Writers need guidance too. According to Libanius (or, more likely, someone writing in the name of the famous tutor of the Emperor Julian), "One could write in the best possible style if he knew what an epistle was, what, generally speaking, custom allowed one to say in it, and into what types it was divided." The handbook of Pseudo-Libanius, *Epistolary Styles* (*Epistolimaioi Charactēres*), is one of two letter-writing manuals that have survived intact. The other is *Epistolary Types* (*Typoi Epistolikoi*), which comes down to us, also erroneously, under the name of Demetrius of Phalerum, a renowned Athenian statesman and orator.[3]

Each manual gives a list of the various letter types available to writers, briefly defines the type, and then provides an example. Pseudo-Demetrius lists twenty-one letter types:

friendly	blaming	consoling
commendatory	reproachful	censorious

2. Adolf Deissmann, *Light from the Ancient East: The New Testament Illustrated by Recently Discovered Texts of the Graeco-Roman World*, trans. Lionel R. M. Strachan, 4th ed. (New York: Doran, 1927), 227–45.

3. Quotations from the letter-writing manuals appearing in this chapter are from Abraham J. Malherbe, *Ancient Epistolary Theorists*, Society of Biblical Literature Sources for Biblical Study 19 (Atlanta: Scholars Press, 1988). Portions of works by Philostratus of Lemnos (*On Letters*), Gregory of Nazianzus (*Epistle* 51), Julius Victor (*The Art of Rhetoric*), and a second Pseudo-Demetrius (*On Style*) are also devoted to epistolary conventions.

admonishing	supplicatory	accusing
threatening	inquiring	apologetic
vituperative	responding	congratulatory
praising	allegorical	ironic
advisory	accounting	thankful

Pseudo-Libanius lists forty-one different types:

parenetic	conciliatory	maligning
blaming	congratulatory	censorious
requesting	contemptuous	inquiring
commending	counteraccusing	encouraging
ironic	replying	consulting
thankful	provoking	declaratory
friendly	consoling	mocking
praying	insulting	submissive
threatening	reporting	enigmatic
denying	angry	suggestive
commanding	diplomatic	grieving
repenting	praising	erotic
reproaching	didactic	mixed
sympathetic	reproving	

Several of the definitions—for example, the threatening style "is that in which we threaten someone," the insulting style "is that in which we insult someone for some reason," and the diplomatic style "is that in which we are diplomatic about something"—are so succinct as to be worthless. Others introduce subtler distinctions. For example, Pseudo-Libanius distinguishes the enigmatic style, "in which some things are said, but others are understood," from the suggestive style, "in which we seem to make a suggestion to someone in response to an inquiry directed to us, while (actually) stamping it with our own aim." The parenetic style, rather than imparting new information to the audience, encourages conventional behaviors and attitudes to which no reasonable person would object. The reproving style differs from the censorious style in that the former is used when someone "denies that he has done something or said something" while the latter censures someone "for what he has done indecently." The closely related blaming style, says Pseudo-Demetrius, "is one that undertakes not to seem harsh." The samples that accompany the definitions are also illuminating because they give a clearer picture of what an ancient writer might say when mocking, repenting, consulting, consoling, blaming, or making an inquiry.

Certain themes show up consistently in these handbooks.[4] A letter is like one-half of a conversation that should "abound in glimpses of character," and, as such, it should not resemble a technical treatise or a political speech (Demetrius, *De elocutione* 223–31). Public and private letters require different styles. Writing in one's own hand is common if the recipient is a close friend. Brevity and clarity are the cardinal virtues of the letter writer, albeit with a few caveats: (1) the length of a letter should suit the purpose and subject, so one should not be "stingy with words when there is much to say" (Gregory of Nazianzus, *Epistle* 51.2); and (2) occasionally, clarity is a secondary concern if the message is meant to be opaque to outsiders (Julius Victor, *Art of Rhetoric* 27). Allusions to history and literature are permissible in moderation. Humor, too, is allowed, if it is appropriate to the mood and audience.

It would be a mistake to think that all letter writers consulted these technical handbooks as they put quill to papyrus. While the advice they contain represents generally recognized protocols, there would be no point in writing them if everyone were already writing letters according to standard operating procedure or "best practices" (just as lots of people fail to floss daily or change their oil every three thousand miles—otherwise, dentists and mechanics would not talk about it so much). That these manuals were copied and ended up surviving suggests that they were widely used, as are the many volumes available today with titles such as *1001 Letters for All Occasions*, *Letter Writing Made Easy!*, *Writing Business Letters for Dummies*, and even *How to Write a Love Letter*. For the most part, epistolary theorists are not setting themselves up as exclusive arbiters of good epistolary taste any more than Ronald Knox sees himself as the special prosecutor of writers who forget to mention crucial clues before the mystery is solved. Rather, they are trying to organize all the different occasions and objectives for writing letters into a system

4. Malherbe, *Ancient Epistolary Theorists*, 12–14.

and offering templates to use in composition. Like the document templates included with word-processing software that assist with the formatting and content of slide shows, contracts, memos, and invoices, the manuals offer shortcuts, so to speak, instead of issuing inflexible rules.

The letter types and styles included by Pseudo-Demetrius and Pseudo-Libanius are found among both the private letters of individuals and the official correspondence produced by and for government functionaries. To a lesser extent, they are also seen in a third category: literary letters. While they borrow many of the same conventions, literary letters are usually longer than private and official letters. Many such letters emerge from educational settings, where students' writing exercises might include imitation of models or impersonation of famous figures such as Hippocrates and Alexander the Great.[5] Others appear to have been written purely for entertainment or for artistic purposes. Horace's letters, composed in hexameter verse for Augustus Caesar, belong under this heading, as do those of Aelian and Alciphron in the early third century CE, which seek nostalgically to re-create the atmosphere of ancient Athens. A number of Greek and Latin writers (e.g., Euripides, Thucydides, Ovid, and Lucian of Samosata) also insert real or fictional letters into histories, tragedies, comedies, or novels, a narrative device also used in the Septuagint (1 Maccabees 12:6–18; 2 Maccabees 1:10–2:18), the New Testament (Acts 15:23–29; 23:26–30; Rev. 2–3), and, much later, movies such as *You've Got Mail* and *Letters from Iwo Jima*.

Literary letters produced in philosophical settings are worthy of attention because of the similarities and differences in form and function one sees when they are placed alongside the New Testament letters.[6] Epicurean, Cynic, and Stoic philosophers used letters to preserve the ideas of a certain teacher, to attract new adherents, to defend their own doctrines or to attack those of another school,

5. M. Luther Stirewalt Jr., *Studies in Ancient Greek Epistolography*, Society of Biblical Literature Resources for Biblical Study 27 (Atlanta: Scholars Press, 1993), 20–22. Students are not the only ones to adopt this practice. In his *Heroides*, the Latin poet Ovid composes letters from famous fictional women (Medea, Briseis, Penelope, Dido) to their husbands and lovers (Jason, Achilles, Odysseus, Aeneas, respectively).

6. Stanley K. Stowers, *Letter Writing in Greco-Roman Antiquity* (Philadelphia: Westminster, 1986), 37–40.

and to exhort their colleagues to live their lives according to their philosophical convictions. These writings resemble essays more than the correspondence found among the papyri. Many of these letters are clearly written under a pseudonym, such as those attributed to Pythagoras, Socrates, Aristotle, Heraclitus, and Apollonius of Tyana, but many others are authentic.

Along with Cicero, Seneca is one of the most prolific writers of philosophical letters in antiquity. He wrote 124 *Moral Epistles* in Latin to his friend Lucilius that stand as classics of the genre. Shortly after the greeting, he launches into a carefully crafted treatise devoted to a particular topic.[7] Especially impressive is the range of topics he can address while emphasizing characteristic Stoic doctrines: saving time (*Epistle* 1), friendship (3), moderation (5), crowds (7), old age (12), holidays (18), practicing what one preaches (20), asthma (54), suicide (70, 77), drunkenness (83), and self-control (116), among others. Although Lucilius was a real person, many scholars doubt that Seneca ever sent him the letters, concluding instead that they are a sort of literary fiction intended for wider circulation from the very beginning.[8] His remark at the start of *Epistle* 75 that his letters are carefree and spontaneous like his conversation, lacking anything "strained or artificial," is surely disingenuous; no one speaks off the cuff quite so elegantly.

Subgenres

The last letter type on the list of Pseudo-Libanius, the "mixed" type, is perhaps the most common, at least among those longer than a paragraph or two. It is not at all unusual for a writer to turn from inquiring to reporting to encouraging in a single letter. Accordingly, it is also common for shorter subgenres to appear within the same document. Paul draws from a number of these shorter literary forms

7. C. S. Lewis's final book, *Letters to Malcolm* (published posthumously in 1964), is a modern example of the same device. Malcolm, unlike Lucilius, is a persona created by Lewis to serve as a sounding board for a series of "letters" considering theological and practical aspects of Christian prayer.
8. Hans-Josef Klauck, *Ancient Letters and the New Testament: A Guide to Context and Exegesis* (Waco: Baylor University Press, 2006), 170–71.

Love Letters, Ancient and Modern

Modern scholars were not the first to realize the importance of ancient letters. The Elizabethan poet and playwright Ben Jonson knew good material when he saw it in the seventy-three fictional *Love Letters* of Philostratus of Lemnos, written early in the third century CE. "Erotic Epistles" would be a better rendering of their Greek title (*epistolae erōtikai*) and more reflective of their content. The first stanza of Jonson's "To Celia" is essentially a translation of portions of Philostratus's *Letter* 33:

> Drink to me only with thine eyes,
> And I will pledge with mine:
> Or leave a kiss but in the cup,
> And I'll not look for wine.

"To Celia" is one of the most beloved poems in the English language, ranking in popularity with the sonnets of Jonson's contemporary, William Shakespeare. Had he found inspiration elsewhere in Philostratus, say, in *Letter* 25 ("to the woman who was not pretty when she was angry") or 37 (in which he begs to be stepped on by the bare foot of his beloved), it probably would not appear in quite as many anthologies.[1]

1. Patricia A. Rosenmeyer, *Ancient Epistolary Fictions: The Letter in Greek Literature* (Cambridge: Cambridge University Press, 2001), 322–29.

---

as he corresponds with his followers.[9] None of the subgenres described below are peculiar to letters.

Blessings and Doxologies

Prayers figure more prominently in early Christian letters than in the ordinary ancient letter on account of the worship setting in which they were read. Blessings and doxologies are two particular types of prayers that regularly appear in Paul's writings. They follow fairly standard forms already established in Jewish practice. Blessings consist of three parts: a reference to God, a description of God as eternally blessed, and a concluding "amen" (Rom. 9:5; 2 Cor. 11:31). Doxologies likewise consist of three parts: a reference to God, a description

9. James L. Bailey and Lyle D. Vander Broek, *Literary Forms in the New Testament: A Handbook* (Louisville: Westminster John Knox, 1992), 21–87.

Letters of Advice

Seneca's practice of couching advice or commentary on a particular topic in the form of letters has proven quite popular. Sometimes the published correspondence begins as real letters exchanged between real persons. More often, the "recipient" consists of a particular demographic. Recent examples span the religious, political, and vocational spectrum, and many of the authors are quite well known:

Letters to a Young Lawyer (Alan M. Dershowitz)
Letters to a Young Catholic (George Weigel)
Letters to a Young Evangelical (Tony Campolo)
Letters to a Young Chef (Daniel Boulud)
The End of America: Letter of Warning to a Young Patriot (Naomi Wolf)
Letters to a Young Contrarian (Christopher Hitchens)
Letters to a Young Gymnast (Nadia Comăneci)
Treatment Kind and Fair: Letters to a Young Doctor (Perri Klass)
Letters to a Young Poet (Rainer Maria Rilke)
Letters to a Young Teacher (Jonathan Kozol)
A Friendly Letter to Skeptics and Atheists (David G. Myers)
Letters to a Young Actor (Robert Sanford Brustein)
Letters to a Buddhist Jew (Akiva Tatz and David Gottlieb)
Letters to a Young Mathematician (Ian Stewart)
Letters to a Young Calvinist (James K. A. Smith)

---

of God as possessing eternal "glory" (*doxa*), and a concluding "amen" (Rom. 11:36; Phil. 4:20). Any embellishment of this basic pattern is noteworthy since it often stands as the first or last phrase that Paul's readers encounter.

Creeds

Creeds are confessions of faith or formal statements of belief. Deuteronomy 6:4 contains the Shema, the best known Jewish creed ("Hear, O Israel: The LORD is our God, the LORD alone"), which Jesus identifies as the first commandment (Mark 12:29). The earliest Christian creed is probably the simple declaration that "Jesus is Lord" (Rom. 10:9). Several passages in the letters are thought to contain or allude to creedal statements (Rom. 1:3–4; 8:34; 1 Cor. 8:6; 1 Tim. 2:5;

47

3:16; 2 Tim. 1:9–10), though Paul rarely makes any explicit point of his quoting a creed. One of the more straightforward examples is in 1 Cor. 15:3–5: "For I handed on to you as of first importance what I in turn had received: that Christ died for our sins in accordance with the scriptures, and that he was buried, and that he was raised on the third day in accordance with the scriptures, and that he appeared to Cephas, then to the twelve." Paul speaks here of "handing on" certain beliefs. He is not claiming to be original. When Paul quotes creedal statements, he is pointing to a foundation he believes he shares with his readers. From this foundation, he can then go on to explore the assumptions or implications of those beliefs: What if Christ were not raised from the dead? What must one also believe or do if one believes in the bodily resurrection? How should one live if Jesus is Lord?

Hymns and Poetry

The earliest descriptions of what Christians did when they gathered together mention hymns (e.g., Acts 16:25; Eph. 5:19; Pliny's letter to Trajan). A hymn is a song in praise of a god. Christians are by no means alone in their use of hymns for religious purposes. Many psalms were intended for recitation in worship. The Dead Sea Scrolls indicate that the Jewish community at Qumran composed and sang hymns as part of its worship. Pagan Greek tradition is also replete with poetry celebrating a deity's powers and other qualities. The *Homeric Hymns*, the *Orphic Hymns*, and the works of Pindar, for example, sing the praises of the gods by listing numerous epithets used to invoke them. Stylistic similarities between these works and early Christian hymns abound. Indeed, much of Cleanthes's *Hymn to Zeus* could be sung without embarrassment by first-century Christians provided they avoid the god's name and the description of his "eternal, two-edged, lightning-forked thunderbolt."

Editors and translators often base decisions about typesetting the text of the letters on their understanding of when Paul is using hymnic material. Because poetic conventions vary so widely between different languages and cultures, however, the use of hymns and poetry in the letters is not self-evident even to those who can read Greek. Rhyming is rare in Greek, and rhythm is difficult to detect unless one hears it performed. The use of some introductory formula is often a clue, as is the presence of figurative language with a lyrical quality that sets it apart from its immediate literary context and the language Paul normally uses (e.g., Eph. 5:14; Phil. 2:6–11; Col. 1:15–20; 1 Tim. 6:15–16; Titus 3:4–7).

Although it is conceivable that Paul himself wrote hymns, most scholars believe that in the hymns he quotes one has access to pre-Pauline ways of thinking and speaking about God and Jesus. Paul expects his audiences to be familiar with his allusions to these hymns, such as the one in Phil. 2:6–11 in which he urges his readers to be like Christ

> who, though he was in the form of God,
> > did not regard equality with God
> > as something to be exploited,
> but emptied himself,
> > taking the form of a slave,
> > being born in human likeness.
> And being found in human form,
> > he humbled himself
> > and became obedient to the point of death—
> > even death on a cross.
> Therefore God also highly exalted him
> > and gave him the name
> > that is above every name,
> so that at the name of Jesus
> > every knee should bend,
> > in heaven and on earth and under the earth,
> and every tongue should confess
> > that Jesus Christ is Lord,
> > to the glory of God the Father.

By quoting it, he is affirming the theology it expresses. Any changes or additions he makes to the familiar wording—perhaps what one sees with the interjection "even death on a cross" between Jesus's descent into human mortality and subsequent ascent to glory—would arrest their attention and underscore his special point of emphasis.

Vice-and-Virtue Lists

When Paul starts talking about the sins people commit, he has a hard time stopping. The wicked who do not acknowledge God are "filled with every kind of wickedness, evil, covetousness, malice. Full of envy, murder, strife, deceit, craftiness, they are gossips, slanderers, God-haters, insolent, haughty, boastful, inventors of evil, rebellious toward parents, foolish, faithless, heartless, ruthless" (Rom. 1:28–31). He is long-winded when it comes to good behavior as well: "The fruit of the Spirit is love, joy, peace, patience, kindness, generosity, faithfulness, gentleness, and self-control" (Gal. 5:22–23).

This habit is not a verbal tic peculiar to Paul. He is making use of the virtue-and-vice list, a literary form common among philosophers in the Hellenistic era. Stoics have a special interest in cataloging virtues and vices, often detailing several categories and subcategories of such qualities as lust and courage. Along with Plato, they ranked prudence, justice, courage, and self-control as the four cardinal virtues. More often, though, the lists are not meant to be systematic or exhaustive. Paul's command to avoid "fornication, impurity, passion, evil desire, and greed" (Col. 3:5), for example, should not be understood as tacit approval of gluttony, pride, or dishonesty. (One apparent exception: it is hard to see what Philo could have possibly omitted when, in *De sacrificiis Abelis et Caini* 32, he says that devotees of pleasure will become unsociable, lawless, slanderous, and fickle, and stops only after he has named 147 separate vices.)

Through repetition and accumulation, virtue-and-vice lists serve a rhetorical function in moral instruction and encouragement. Living well is not just a matter of theory but of practice. Virtue-and-vice lists provide concrete examples of how to lead a moral life. It is not enough to say, "Be good!" It is more effective to list seven deadly sins to avoid, or to encourage obedience to a "law" stating that a Boy Scout is trustworthy, loyal, helpful, friendly, courteous, kind, obedient, cheerful, thrifty, brave, clean, and reverent. The lists reinforce conventional moral standards rather than aiming at originality. They typically apply to a general audience. On occasion they are tailored to a specific group or circumstance, as in Dio Chrysostom's treatises on the qualities of a good king (*Orations* 1.13; 2.75; 62.2). Over two dozen such lists appear in Paul's letters, mostly general in nature (Rom.

13:13; 2 Tim. 3:2–5) but some applicable only to certain situations (1 Cor. 6:9–10; 1 Tim. 3:2–3; Titus 1:7–8).

Household Codes

Scholars use the term "household code" to refer to lists of duties within the context of household relationships. Such lists are found as early as Aristotle and are common in Hellenistic literature (Aristotle, *Politica* 1253b, 1259b; Seneca, *Epistle* 94.1; Josephus, *Against Apion* 2.201–7). Household codes take various forms but usually govern reciprocal relations between (1) husbands and wives, (2) fathers and children, and (3) masters and slaves. Maintaining proper relations in the household was thought to be necessary for maintaining order in society as a whole. For this reason, the inclusion of household codes may serve apologetic purposes by showing the dominant culture that group membership is perfectly compatible with being a good citizen (as in Dionysius of Halicarnassus, *Antiquitates romanae* 2.24.3–2.27.4).

The New Testament contains a number of household codes (Eph. 5:21–6:9; Col. 3:18–4:1; 1 Tim. 2:8–15; 6:1–2; Titus 2:1–10; 3:1–7; 1 Pet. 2:13–3:7). Each has been Christianized in some fashion and has its own distinctive emphases. Colossians has more to say to slaves. Ephesians, which is read at many weddings today, expands upon marital relations. The male-centered, hierarchical character of the codes offends the sensibilities of many modern readers. Some scholars note that the form they take in the New Testament, when compared with other ancient examples, occupies a middle ground on the spectrum between patriarchy and egalitarianism.

Chiasm

Chiasm is a literary form usually associated with biblical poetry that consists of reverse parallelism. Two or more phrases or ideas appear and are then repeated in the opposite order. In 1 Cor. 11:8–12, the first, second, fourth, and fifth lines exhibit this structure internally, as does the passage as a whole:

A Indeed, man was not made from woman, but woman from man.

B Neither was man created for the sake of woman, but woman
for the sake of man.

C For this reason a woman ought to have a symbol of authority on her head, because of the angels.

B' Nevertheless, in the Lord woman is not independent of man
or man independent of woman.

A' For just as woman came from man, so man comes through
woman; but all things come from God.

The use of chiasm achieves a pleasing rhetorical effect and also serves
as an aid to memory. Recognition of chiasm can be helpful in marking
out where one thought unit ends and another begins. Comparison of
the parallel elements, which are typically similar though not always
strictly synonymous, generates clues as to the intended significance
of the specific language Paul uses. When the number of elements is
odd, the focal idea of the passage is found at the "center."

Classifying Paul's Letters

It is difficult to envision Paul sitting down with a dog-eared copy of
Pseudo-Demetrius or Pseudo-Libanius as he scolds the Galatians or
answers questions posed by the Corinthians. Elements of most of
the letter types listed in the handbooks are nevertheless present in
his letters. These types are akin to the basic chords, rhythms, and
harmonies that a skilled musician varies, builds on, amplifies, and
inverts in improvisational jazz. However spontaneous it may sound,
they do not create new music out of thin air or without mastery of
the fundamentals. Paul is likewise fluent in the fundamentals of letter
writing. The way he manipulates, combines, conforms to, or subverts
the familiar genres and subgenres displays his literary virtuosity.

To later readers it may not be obvious that a particular letter aims
at expressing sympathy or contempt or gratitude. By noting resem-
blances to the examples in the handbooks, one may discover more
than initially meets the eye in a Pauline letter. This is the true value
of the epistolary theorists for readers of Paul. Classification for classification's sake is of little use, all the more so since Paul's letters are

all of the mixed type. Keeping in mind these letter genres and the types of things people did via letters leads to sharper questions about what Paul is trying to accomplish as he writes. It also enables the interpreter to make finer and more sophisticated distinctions when sorting through the possible answers.

Romans

In length, content, and tone, Romans resembles an essay as much as a letter. Insofar as it reflects a particular setting, however, it is appropriate to treat it as a real, if anomalous, letter that seeks to accomplish multiple tasks.

The immediate occasion for writing Romans is Paul's plan to travel to Spain to spread the gospel (15:20–29). Hoping to stop in Rome on the way, he writes to seek their help. Romans 16 includes a recommendation or introduction for Phoebe (16:1–2) as she delivers the letter to various gatherings in the capital city. It also serves in part as a self-commendation intended to secure the aid of the Roman Christians, most of whom have never met Paul. His reputation may be the source of some trepidation in Rome, all the more so if he is seeking their financial assistance. Controversy connected to his mission and message accounts for the features of Romans found in many apologetic letters. From several quarters, the gentile mission met with objections. Paul produces a series of arguments, examples, and counterarguments in support of his view that Jews and gentiles alike are made righteous by faith and not by works of the law. There would be no need for so elaborate a defense of this idea if everyone accepted it as a matter of course.

Conciliatory letters usually aim at repairing relations with someone whom the author has caused grief or sorrow. Paul himself does not appear to have offended the readers, but there is palpable tension between different factions that he wants to ease. The church in Rome includes both Jews and gentiles as members. Mutual suspicion and antipathy between these groups did not magically disappear when they uttered the words "Jesus is Lord." This letter, especially Rom. 9–11, makes an extended appeal to Jews and gentiles to acknowledge that they both belong to God's elect on the same terms. A transition

occurs at 12:1 between this didactic portion of the letter and a parenetic section with concrete instructions designed to help the Roman
Christians live in harmony. The scruples of members Paul labels "the
weak," who abstain from meat and wine and celebrate special holy
days, annoy or embarrass "the strong," who regard such observances
as self-righteous or superstitious. (It is not clear whether "the strong"
and "the weak" are synonyms for gentile and Jew.) Paul urges them to
be patient with one another and not pass judgment on matters where
persons of good faith can have legitimate disagreements.

1 Corinthians

The Corinthians have written to Paul, and 1 Corinthians contains
his answers. In this respect, it is an example of the responding letter,
with Paul's responses signaled by the phrase "now concerning" (7:1,
25; 8:1; 12:1; 16:1, 12). Each response could stand by itself as a letter in
the advisory style. According to Pseudo-Libanius, the advisory style is
similar to parenesis but differs in that parenesis is "speech that does not
admit of a counter-statement," while advice leaves room for debate.
When Paul deals with their questions about marriage and sexuality,
food sacrificed to idols, and the use of spiritual gifts in the assembly,
he is confronting issues for which the relevance of Jesus's death and
resurrection may not be self-evident to an objective observer. On many
points, Paul's position is firm and unambiguous. On others, however,
he concedes that he lacks a warrant for a hard and fast rule. "I have
no command of the Lord," he says when addressing the situation of
betrothed virgins (7:25). Variations of this formula appear elsewhere
(7:6, 12, 35; 11:16).

In addition to his responses to their questions, Paul addresses several
matters that have come to his attention only by way of Chloe (1:11).
His handling of these affairs alternates between different epistolary
styles. First Corinthians 2–4, in which Paul discusses the divisions
created by their allegiance to different teachers, features elements
of self-recommendation (for Paul's special status as their founder),
mocking and irony (3:16–20; 4:8), threats (4:21: "What would you
prefer? Am I to come to you with a stick?"), and admonition (4:14).
Standard parenetic strategies are on display in his use of rhetorical

questions to which he already knows the answer (3:16; cf. 5:6; 6:2–3, 9, 15–19; 9:13, 24).

Paul's language is stronger when he turns to their toleration of incest (1 Cor. 5) and their improper behavior when celebrating the Lord's Supper (11:17–34). His manner conforms to the censorious and commanding styles in both cases. In the former, he reinforces his instructions with a brief vice list, while he quotes at length from a liturgical tradition associated with the Last Supper to bring them to their senses in the latter.

2 Corinthians

Whether or not one sees the present form of 2 Corinthians as a compilation of multiple letters—numbering anywhere from two to six, according to many scholars—it is obvious that it combines multiple epistolary types and styles. Doubts about Paul's familiarity with the form and function of various letter types, furthermore, are put to rest by his own commentary: "Are we beginning to commend ourselves again? Surely we do not need, as some do, letters of recommendation to you or from you, do we? You yourselves are our letter, written on our hearts, to be known and read by all" (3:1–2). Other teachers appear to have cast aspersions on Paul for his failure to produce any letters of recommendation. Who is Paul, who vouches for him, and by what authority does he exercise authority over you? These questions demand a response. Paul challenges the notion that recommendation letters are necessary or sufficient for determining who is and is not an authentic minister of God. Although he says, "We are not commending ourselves to you again" (5:12; cf. 3:1; 4:2; 10:18), in reality he protests too much. The better part of the book (2:14–7:4) constitutes an elaborate self-recommendation for anyone who might wonder about his understanding of Christian ministry.

Second Corinthians 10–13 complements this self-recommendation, though more in the style of the apologetic or accounting letters. These closely related types aim respectively to provide a defense by countering charges that have been made or to give reasons something has not taken place. Both types seek to clear up a misunderstanding. Paul explains his travel plans in 1:15–2:13, but it is in the final chapters that his apologetic motives are most conspicuous (cf. 12:19: "Have you been thinking all along that we have been defending ourselves before you?"). Not only does he defend himself against charges that he is weak and uninspiring (10:10; 11:6); he goes so far as to boast repeatedly that his modus operandi gives evidence of true power and spirit. Present also in 2 Cor. 10–13 are elements of counteraccusation against those who have undermined him (10:10–12; 11:12–15), irony (12:13, and perhaps in his reference to his opponents as "super-apostles"), threats (13:3, 10), and reproach for the personal offense caused by the Corinthians despite all of Paul's efforts on their behalf (11:1–11).

Between the arguments that open and close the letter, one finds a conciliatory letter (7:5–13) and a letter of request (2 Cor. 8–9), where Paul discusses the collection he is taking up for the poor in Jerusalem. His tone throughout these chapters, so different from those that follow, shows that he is sincere when he says that he is requesting and not commanding (8:8–10).

Galatians

Galatians offers more firsthand information about Paul's life and ministry than any other letter. However valuable this data may be, the purpose of the autobiographical section in 1:10–2:21 is not to serve as a source for reconstructing Paul's apostolic career. Rather, it functions as a spirited apology in the face of accusations that he is leading his followers astray. Far from groveling and begging for forgiveness, he recounts charges made against him, offers a vigorous defense of his conduct, and turns the tables on his opponents in the style of the counteraccusing letter. The counteraccusations are not leveled against the Galatians themselves, yet his remarks about the Judaizers who want to compel gentile believers to undergo circumcision are clearly intended for their instruction.

Much of the letter (3:1–5:12) is didactic in nature. This provides the scriptural and theological basis for the parenesis that takes up the final section (5:13–6:10). Interspersed with this teaching and exhortation are comments that correspond to elements of several related letter types. In the way he bemoans their departure from the gospel he himself has taught them, reproach is the dominant mode (3:1–5;

4:8–11; 5:1–3, 7–12). He maligns the integrity of those who preach "a different gospel" and warns the Galatians against following them into error (1:6–10; 2:11–14). The admonishing style adopted by Paul seeks to assign blame for some shortcoming with an eye toward altering the thinking and behavior of the party on the receiving end of the censure. The distinctions between these letter types and styles as described in the handbooks can be subtle: for example, when Paul says of those who are troubling the Galatians, "I wish they would go the whole way and emasculate themselves" (5:12 New International Version), is he operating in the mocking style or the insulting style, or is he simply angry?

Only a close friend elicits the fierce emotion Paul pours out here. It is no surprise, then, to also find basic features of the friendly letter as he recalls good times in the past, reiterates his desire to benefit the Galatians, and expresses longing for a reunion with his absent comrades.

Ephesians

Of the thirteen letters attributed to Paul, Ephesians has the fewest epistolary features. It likely originated as a circular letter sent to several churches in western Asia Minor and resembles a treatise or essay more than a letter. Portions of it read like a letter of congratulation for gentiles "who once were far off" but have been brought near by the blood of Christ and now enjoy a new identity as part of the people of Israel's God (2:11–22). The second half of Ephesians is largely parenetic in nature, filled with uncontroversial ethical admonitions pertaining to matters inside and outside the household.

Philippians

As with 2 Corinthians, the question of genre for Philippians is connected to the question of literary integrity. Many scholars—fewer, though, than for 2 Corinthians—believe that Philippians in its present form has been stitched together with excerpts from three separate letters. Abrupt shifts in tone or subject at 3:2 and 4:10 seem to support this thesis. Philippians is hardly unique among Paul's letters in this respect. This letter, too, is of the mixed type, which probably accounts for the rough transitions.

Philippians is, first, a letter of friendship. Recollection of the origins of the friendship and shared experiences (1:30; 4:15) is a regular motif in such letters, as is the emphasis on the way in which writing attempts to overcome the pain of being apart (1:8, 27; 2:12). Paul's concern for their well-being is evident (1:9–11; 2:19; 4:19). At the same time, Paul is confident that they feel the same way (1:7, 19; 2:2; 4:10). Second, Philippians is a letter of thanksgiving. The Philippians have sent him a generous financial gift, for which he expresses gratitude (4:10–20). Third, the letter clearly functions as a commendation for Timothy and Epaphroditus, two of Paul's trusted emissaries who are on their way to Philippi. Paul may have included the self-recommendation in 1:12–26 just in case any of his readers are having second thoughts about their association with someone who spends so much time in jail.

Throughout the letter are various exhortations characteristic of the parenetic letter (1:27–28; 2:3–5, 12–15; 3:17; 4:1–3). Warnings about "the dogs, . . . the evil workers, . . . those who mutilate the flesh" (3:2) highlight negative examples and incorporate aspects of the maligning letter.

Colossians

The primary impetus for Colossians is the author's worry that the readers will be led astray "through philosophy and empty deceit" (2:4, 8, 16–23). His response incorporates elements of the denying style as he offers a series of counterarguments to those of his opponents, who are never identified and whose views are only vaguely described. The theological foundation for his rebuttal of these teachings is found in the stately hymn he quotes at length (1:15–20), emphasizing and celebrating the cosmic dimensions of Jesus's messianic identity. Much of the letter consists of parenesis in the form of vice-and-virtue lists (3:5–8, 12), a household code (3:18–4:1), and general admonitions.

1 Thessalonians

First Thessalonians begins as a friendly letter and ends as a letter of consolation (4:13–5:11) and parenesis (5:12–22). Paul heaps praise on the Thessalonians for their steadfast faith and love in the first two chapters. As in other friendly letters, he does this in the course of remembering their time together before he left the city (1:4–2:16), regretting the geographic distance that now separates them (2:17–20), and expressing his earnest desire for news of their situation (3:1–10). Since their last meeting, some of their members have died. The death of a loved one always causes grief. This emotion has been magnified by the Thessalonians' fear that the dearly departed will be out of luck when Jesus returns. "But we do not want you to be uninformed . . . about those who have died," Paul writes, "so that you may not grieve as others do" (4:13). His teaching about Christ's return aims to console them for their loss and ease their minds about the fate of the deceased. He invites them to offer one another the same encouragement (4:18; 5:11).

2 Thessalonians

The primary objective of 2 Thessalonians is twofold. First, the didactic objective of 2:1–12 has to do with the audience's misunderstanding of Paul's teaching about the end times in 1 Thessalonians. To the extent that the author sees their situation not as a misunderstanding but as the result of deception in the form of a forged letter, there are also elements of the maligning letter. Second, the expectation of Christ's imminent return has led some of the Thessalonians to stop working. In 3:6–13 Paul admonishes them for their idleness, a problem he thought he had already solved with earlier instructions. Repetition of the verb "command" (3:4, 6, 10, 12) suggests that this letter of admonition might just as easily be considered a letter of command.

1 Timothy

A majority of scholars view the Pastoral Epistles (1–2 Timothy and Titus) as a multipart pseudonymous document written several decades after Paul's death. The genre of 1 Timothy in this view is an early form of "church orders" seen in the second century and later in such writings as *Didache* and *Didascalia Apostolorum*. The purpose of these later texts is to govern communal affairs in the church. If 1 Timothy is any indication, the community in question is certainly in need of order, and the author seeks to provide it by adapting household code material to the church family (3:15). The prevalence of the word "command" (1:3, 5, 18; 4:11; 5:7; 6:13–14, 17) suggests that the commanding letter mentioned by Pseudo-Libanius is an apt designation.

In this vein, some suggest a specific type of letter, the *mandata principis* ("commandments of the ruler"), as the best way to categorize 1 Timothy.[10] Letters in this genre are a variety of royal or bureaucratic correspondence sent by a superior to a representative and contain instructions on the representative's mission. The audience of such letters includes the newly appointed delegate, who receives needed validation from the superior, and also the constituency to which he has been sent, who then have some means by which to assess the performance of the delegate. Whether or not one regards Paul as the true author, the use of plural pronouns (e.g., 6:20) in a letter ostensibly sent to a private individual fits with the genre.

2 Timothy

Scholars who regard the Pastoral Epistles as a composition produced after the apostle's death see 2 Timothy as a farewell discourse or "last will and testament" that brings his career to a fitting literary conclusion. Second Temple Judaism features many such examples of the testamentary genre. Inspired by the story of the dying Jacob in Gen. 49, works such as *Testaments of the Twelve Patriarchs* and *Testament of Job* depict an aged figure reflecting on his life and offering ethical advice to a younger generation.

Notwithstanding the presence of testamentary elements, 2 Timothy is nevertheless cast in the form of a letter with striking similarities to the personal parenetic letter described in the handbooks. Personal parenetic letters put forward models for emulation (1:3–2:13; 3:10–11; 4:16–18) and exhort the reader to pursue virtue and eschew vice (3:2–5). The author wants Timothy to "always be sober, endure suffering, do the work of an evangelist, carry out [his] ministry fully"

10. Luke Timothy Johnson, *The First and Second Letters to Timothy*, Anchor Bible 35A (New York: Doubleday, 2001), 139–42.

(4:5). Toward this end, he also employs elements of the maligning letter to highlight negative examples (1:15; 2:16–18; 3:1–9; 4:14–15).

Titus

The question of genre is the same for Titus as for 1 Timothy. In addition, warnings about "rebellious people, idle talkers and deceivers" (1:10–16) incorporate elements of the maligning letter. Comparisons are occasionally made between the Pastoral Epistles and *prosōpopoiia*, an ancient rhetorical device often used as a school exercise. *Prosōpopoiia* is "speech in character" or the literary impersonation of a well-known figure. If the Pastoral Epistles constitute such an exercise, their author—totally unsuspected for over seventeen centuries—surely deserves high marks.

Philemon

Even this shortest of the letters serves multiple purposes. The details of what Paul wants from Philemon may be hazy, but this is clearly a letter of request or supplication. Paul explicitly states that he is not commanding (8–9, 14). He is sending Onesimus, a fugitive slave who has become a Christian, back to his owner and is requesting some special treatment for him. The delicate nature of the situation probably explains the letter's diplomatic character.

At the same time, the letter functions as a recommendation for Onesimus. Such letters usually arise out of a positive relationship between sender and recipient and concern a third party. Reminders of the ties that bind them in Christian friendship are scattered throughout the letter to Philemon. Fitting this letter into the framework of the patronage system is tricky: Is Paul the patron on account of his status as spiritual mentor, or is he the client on account of financial support he may have received from Philemon? And what role do Apphia and Archippus, the other named recipients, play? Julius Victor says that recommendations "should be written truthfully or not at all" (*Art of Rhetoric* 27). Those who write and read such letters today know that this rule is all too often broken, as it must have been in antiquity (or else there would be no need to state it). That the letter has survived may be a sign of Paul's sincerity and Philemon's compliance with Paul's request.

Conclusion

From this survey it is possible to make a few generalizations. First, with very few exceptions, Paul's letters qualify as occasional literature; that is, they are written in response to specific occasions or circumstances. Even if their content transcends the original occasion prompting them, the letters do not originate as abstract essays or treatises. Paul is not a writer in search of a topic. His topics find him, so to speak. Were it not for the enthusiastic and unexpected response of gentiles to his proclamation of the risen Jesus and the conflicts it generated, it has been argued, Paul might never have formulated his signature doctrine, justification by faith.

Second, most of the letters contain healthy servings of parenesis. Parenesis is a general term for exhortation and advice usually relating to moral behavior. It is important to keep in mind when reading Paul's letters that parenetic discourse reinforces principles with which the audience already agrees.[11] It functions as a reminder of what they already know or ought to know (cf. 1 Thess. 2:1–11). When Paul condemns fornication or greed or idolatry, then, he is not introducing novel ideas. He may give theological arguments to buttress this exhortation, but just as often he is comfortable stringing together a series of instructions with little comment (as in Rom. 12:9–21). Paul wants his readers to practice what they preach, as the saying goes. In this he himself is actually practicing what was preached by Hellenistic philosophers like Dio Chrysostom, who says that "it is not our ignorance of the difference between good and evil that hurts us so much as it is our failure to heed the dictates of reason . . . and be true to our personal opinions," and so it is not superfluous "to remind men of this without ceasing" (*Orations* 17.2).

Third, most of the letters to varying degrees exhibit features of the friendly letter. No doubt this is because, in many cases, Paul and his readers have formed a close friendship over time. Friends feel free to say things they have said before, as Paul does in the parenetic sections of his letters. In some cases it is less apparent that they have forged such a bond. According to Pseudo-Demetrius, the friendly letter

---

11. Abraham J. Malherbe, *Moral Exhortation: A Greco-Roman Sourcebook*, Library of Early Christianity 4 (Philadelphia: Westminster, 1986), 124–25.

"seems to be written by a friend to a friend." "But," he continues, "it is by no means (only) friends who write (in this manner)." It is not unusual to write as though a friend to an individual one has never met. Where Paul and his readers are not yet friends, the act of writing itself cultivates a closer relationship. While it may be an exaggeration to claim that a letter's contents are "less significant than the very fact of its existence," simply taking the trouble to write in the first place is a token of friendship, especially given the logistics of letter writing and delivery in the first century.[12]

This chapter focused on the Greco-Roman epistolographical background of the letters because distinctively Jewish letter-writing customs appear to have had relatively little influence on Paul. The closest parallels to Paul among surviving Jewish letters come from Josephus and other hellenized Jews who, like Paul, draw deeply from the well of Greco-Roman literary tradition. Early Christian writers do adopt the Jewish practice of sending encyclical letters (e.g., Acts 15:22–35; 28:21). Jewish authorities in Palestine used encyclicals to communicate with Diaspora synagogues to standardize the observance of holy days and for other reasons.[13] In a twist of fate, the father of Christian epistolography is carrying just such a letter when he sets off for Damascus to persecute the followers of Jesus (Acts 9:1–2).

It was natural for Paul, a hellenized Jew, to borrow Greco-Roman literary forms in corresponding with his friends and followers. These forms help him say what he needs to say. Form, however, does not trump content. Paul uses Greco-Roman genres as a vehicle to deliver Jewish content, such as the idea of a messiah and an apocalyptic view of history, just as the Gospels resemble yet differ in significant ways from ancient biographies. This imperfect match of form and substance accounts for the similarities and the dissimilarities between Paul and his pagan counterparts.

12. See Carol Poster, "A Conversation Halved: Epistolary Theory in Greco-Roman Antiquity," in *Letter-Writing Manuals and Instruction from Antiquity to the Present*, ed. C. Poster and L. C. Mitchell (Columbia: University of South Carolina Press, 2007), 27.

13. David E. Aune, *The New Testament in Its Literary Environment*, Library of Early Christianity 8 (Philadelphia: Westminster, 1987), 179–80.

For Further Discussion

1. Which of Paul's letters appear to fit within the categories of epistolary genres found in the handbooks of Pseudo-Demetrius and Pseudo-Libanius? Does Paul show any awareness of any of these specific genres?
2. Are Paul's letters letters or epistles?
3. For which of the disputed letters are questions about genre and authorship most closely related?

For Further Reading

Aune, David E. *The New Testament in Its Literary Environment*. Library of Early Christianity 8. Philadelphia: Westminster, 1987.

Bailey, James L., and Lyle D. Vander Broek. *Literary Forms in the New Testament: A Handbook*. Louisville: Westminster John Knox, 1992.

Dahl, Nils A. "Letter." In *The Interpreter's Dictionary of the Bible: Supplementary Volume*, edited by Keith Crim et al., 538–41. Nashville: Abingdon, 1976.

Deissmann, Adolf. *Light from the Ancient East: The New Testament Illustrated by Recently Discovered Texts of the Graeco-Roman World*. Translated by Lionel R. M. Strachan. 4th ed. New York: Doran, 1927. Reprinted, Grand Rapids: Baker, 1965.

Doty, William G. *Letters in Primitive Christianity*. Guides to Biblical Scholarship 7. Philadelphia: Fortress, 1973.

Malherbe, Abraham J. *Ancient Epistolary Theorists*. Society of Biblical Literature Sources for Biblical Study 19. Atlanta: Scholars Press, 1988.

———, ed. *The Cynic Epistles: A Study Edition*. Society of Biblical Literature Sources for Biblical Study 12. Missoula, MT: Scholars Press, 1977.

Murphy-O'Connor, Jerome. *Paul the Letter-Writer: His World, His Options, His Skills*. Good News Studies 41. Collegeville, MN: Michael Glazier/Liturgical Press, 1995.

Poster, Carol. "A Conversation Halved: Epistolary Theory in Greco-Roman Antiquity." In *Letter-Writing Manuals and Instruction from Antiquity to the Present*, edited by C. Poster and L. C. Mitchell, 21–51. Columbia: University of South Carolina Press, 2007.

Stirewalt, M. Luther, Jr. *Paul, the Letter Writer*. Grand Rapids: Eerdmans, 2003.

———. *Studies in Ancient Greek Epistolography*. Society of Biblical Literature Resources for Biblical Study 27. Atlanta: Scholars Press, 1993.

Stowers, Stanley K. *Letter Writing in Greco-Roman Antiquity*. Library of Early Christianity 5. Philadelphia: Westminster, 1986.

————. "Letters (Greek and Latin)." In *The Anchor Bible Dictionary*, edited by David Noel Freedman et al., 4:290–93. New York: Doubleday, 1992.

White, John L. "Ancient Greek Letters." In *Greco-Roman Literature and the New Testament: Selected Forms and Genres*, edited by David E. Aune, 85–105. Society of Biblical Literature Sources for Biblical Study 21. Atlanta: Scholars Press, 1988.

————. *Light from Ancient Letters*. Philadelphia: Fortress, 1986.

3

How Paul Writes

Organizing a Letter and Making an Argument

Letters belong to different genres on the basis of the aims their authors seek to achieve. All letters of every genre seek to achieve some aim, even the shortest missives among the papyrus documents found in Roman Egypt. It may be as trivial as a man's complaint to the police that someone has stolen his pig from his doorstep (Rylands Papyrus 140). Or it may be only to relay a small amount of information, as when a student writes to assure his father that he is studying hard and taking care of his health (Oxyrhynchus Papyrus 1296). Whatever the genre or purpose, letters also exhibit consistent structural features. Indeed, the form it takes is the key clue that a document is in fact a letter and not, say, a movie script, affidavit, or poem.

A preliminary observation about epistolary structure is in order for modern readers of Paul's letters: However Paul may have gone about organizing his letters, it is certain that he did not organize them into chapters and verses. The chapter-and-verse format of the biblical writings originated centuries later. Stephen Langton, a Parisian professor who later became archbishop of Canterbury, first introduced early in the thirteenth century the chapter divisions now in use. Verse divisions for the New Testament books first appear in the 1551 Greek and Latin edition of Robert Stephanus. According to his son, Stephanus worked out the verse divisions on horseback as he traveled from Paris to Lyons, leading many to hypothesize that his occasionally idiosyncratic decisions were the result of his horse stumbling.[1]

These chapter and verse divisions are extremely useful when making reference to specific texts for the purpose of commentary. It is not necessary to pay close attention to them, however, to read Paul's letters as he meant for them to be read. His first readers—indeed, most readers until the sixteenth century—never experienced his letters in this form. The divisions often correspond quite well to the flow of thought. But in many instances, chapter and verse breaks fall at unnatural, arbitrary, even misleading points that disrupt or distort Paul's argument. For example, Col. 4 begins with the command to masters to treat their slaves justly. This gives the impression that the behavior of slave owners stands at the start of a new section when in reality it is the last in a series of instructions on household duties of husbands, wives, children, and slaves going back to 3:18. A chapter division at Eph. 6:1 breaks up a similar list of duties for no apparent reason. Having heard it read at so many weddings, it may be difficult to read 1 Cor. 13 as part of a larger discussion of spiritual gifts like speaking in tongues and their function within the body of Christ, especially when it is artificially sequestered from the chapters before and after it.

Another example from 1 Corinthians further illustrates the way in which slavish adherence to the chapter and verse divisions can lead readers astray. The NRSV of 1 Cor. 14:33–36 reads as follows:

> for God is a God not of disorder but of peace.
>
> (As in all the churches of the saints, women should be silent in the churches. For they are not permitted to speak, but should be subordinate, as the law also says. If there is anything they desire to know, let them ask their husbands at home. For it is shameful for a woman to speak in church. Or did the word of God originate with you? Or are you the only ones it has reached?)

1. Bruce M. Metzger, *Manuscripts of the Greek Bible: An Introduction to Greek Palaeography* (Oxford: Oxford University Press, 1981), 41–42.

The NRSV translators believe that the first part of 14:33 belongs grammatically with 14:32—to form a complete sentence: "And the spirits of prophets are subject to the prophets, for God is a God not of disorder but of peace." The second half of 14:33 then starts both a new sentence and new paragraph. On the other hand, the KJV reads 14:33 as a grammatical unit: "For God is not the author of confusion, but of peace, as in all the churches of the saints." What difference does it make? If the traditional versification is grammatically accurate, then Paul is citing what happens "in all the churches" as a precedent for his advice to the Corinthians regarding prophecy and speaking in tongues. If the NRSV translators are correct, then Paul is claiming that female silence is the norm "in all the churches." Editors who wish to produce an English translation that says what the author wanted to say must make typographical decisions about whether or where to add subheadings or downplay chapter and verse breaks when they prepare Bible versions for publication.

Reading an Ancient Manuscript

Ancient documents differ from modern documents in a number of ways. In the first century, standard handwriting featured little or no punctuation or even divisions between words. Galatians 1:20–23 would have looked something like this:

INWHATIAMWRITINGTOYOUBEFOREGODIDONOTLIETHENIWENTINTO
THEREGIONSOFSYRIAANDCILICIAANDIWASSTILLUNKNOWNBYSIGHT
TOTHECHURCHESOFJUDEATHATAREINCHRISTTHEYONLYHEARD
ITSAIDTHEONEWHOFORMERLYWASPERSECUTINGUSISNOWPROCLAIM
INGTHEFAITHHEONCETRIEDTODESTROY

A modern version looks like this, from the NRSV:

In what I am writing to you, before God, I do not lie! Then I went into the regions of Syria and Cilicia, and I was still unknown by sight to the churches of Judea that are in Christ; they only heard it said, "The one who formerly was persecuting us is now proclaiming the faith he once tried to destroy."

This explains in part why modern scholars sometimes disagree about how the text should read.

What sort of scheme did Paul use if he did not organize his letters into chapters and verses? The short answer is obvious. Scholars note that ancient letters have a three-part structure: (1) opening/prescript, (2) body, and (3) closing. This standard structure can be seen when juxtaposing two examples, one from the New Testament (Acts 15:23–29) and one from a third-century BCE papyrus:[2]

Acts 15:23–29	Zenon Papyrus (Cairo) 59426
Opening	
The brothers, both the apostles and the elders, to the believers of Gentile origin in Antioch and Syria and Cilicia, greetings.	Dromon to Zenon, greeting.
Body	
Since we have heard that certain persons who have gone out from us, though with no instructions from us, have said things to disturb you and have unsettled your minds, we have decided unanimously to choose representatives and send them to you, along with our beloved Barnabas and Paul, who have risked their lives for the sake of our Lord Jesus Christ. We have therefore sent Judas and Silas, who themselves will tell you the same things by word of mouth. For it has seemed good to the Holy Spirit and to us to impose on you no further burden than these essentials: that you abstain from what has been sacrificed to idols and from blood and from what is strangled and from fornication. If you keep yourselves from these, you will do well.	I give thanks to all the gods if you are in good health yourself and everything else has been satisfactory. I too am well, and in accordance with what you wrote to me I am taking the utmost care that no one troubles your people. When you are ready to sail up in good health, order one of your people to buy a cotyla of Attic honey; for I require it for my eyes by order of the god.
Closing	
Farewell.	[none]

With the exception of Philemon, Paul's letters are longer than the typical Hellenistic letter, but they contain the same basic components.

This chapter will first discuss the conventions seen in letter openings and closings. Recognition of the literary habits found in these sections adds to the reader's appreciation of what Paul is trying to

2. A. S. Hunt and C. C. Edgar, *Select Papyri*, Loeb Classical Library (London: Heinemann, 1932), 1:273–75.

accomplish. The main substance of his letters is of course found in the body. Discussion of the body will focus on the rhetorical patterns and strategies by which Paul makes his arguments and formulates his theology.

Beginning a Letter

It is possible to set a tone and send a message in the first few words of a letter, as when Sigmund Freud started addressing Carl Jung as "Dear Dr. Jung"—eschewing the "Dear friend" he had used previously—after a public dispute over certain aspects of psychoanalytic theory.[3] At the same time, it is possible to misinterpret such fleeting phrases. Much was made of Ronald Reagan often beginning letters to his wife, Nancy, with the salutation "Dear Mommie" when they were published shortly after his death. Is this evidence of a twisted, Freudian relationship between the former president and first lady? Probably not. For many couples who have raised children, the habit of calling each other "Mommie" and "Daddy" proves hard to break. As Freud himself once observed, "Sometimes a cigar is just a cigar" and not a sign of or a symbol for something else.

Familiarity with the standard components of the Hellenistic letter greeting helps to prevent such misunderstandings. Ancient letters begin with a prescript. The prescript includes the name of the sender, the recipient(s), and a salutation, which usually consists of the single word *chairein* (Greek) or *salus* (Latin), as in these examples:

Apion to Didymus, greetings. (Tebtunis Papyrus 421)

Thais to her Tigrios, greetings. (Oxyrhynchus Papyrus 932)

Cicero to Atticus, greetings. (Cicero, *Epistulae ad Atticum* 10.2)

On occasion, a phrase describing the author or addressee appears:

Apollonius to Ptolemaeus his father, greetings! (Paris Papyrus 47)

3. Thomas Mallon, *Yours Ever: People and Their Letters* (New York: Pantheon, 2009), 242.

> To Julius Domitius, military tribune of the legion, from Aurelius Archelaus, his *beneficiarius*, greetings. (Oxyrhynchus Papyrus 32)

> James, a servant of God and of the Lord Jesus Christ,
>> To the twelve tribes in the Dispersion:
>> Greetings. (James 1:1)

> To my lady and beloved aunt from Tare, daughter of your sister Allous, greetings from God. (Papyrus Bouriant 25)

Lengthy elaboration in the address is less common among Greek and Latin letter writers than it is in the New Testament (see especially 1–2 Peter and 2 John).

In his tendency to expand the greeting well beyond the bare minimum, Paul resembles his fellow Christian authors:

> Paul, a servant of Jesus Christ, called to be an apostle, set apart for the gospel of God, which he promised beforehand through his prophets in the holy scriptures, the gospel concerning his Son, who was descended from David according to the flesh and was declared to be Son of God with power according to the spirit of holiness by resurrection from the dead, Jesus Christ our Lord, through whom we have received grace and apostleship to bring about the obedience of faith among all Gentiles for the sake of his name, including yourselves who are called to belong to Jesus Christ,
>> To all God's beloved in Rome, who are called to be saints:
>> Grace to you and peace from God our Father and the Lord Jesus Christ. (Rom. 1:1–7)

> Paul, called to be an apostle of Christ Jesus by the will of God, and our brother Sosthenes,
>> To the church of God that is in Corinth, to those who are sanctified in Christ Jesus, called to be saints, together with all those who in every place call on the name of our Lord Jesus Christ, both their Lord and ours:
>> Grace to you and peace from God our Father and the Lord Jesus Christ. (1 Cor. 1:1–2)

> Paul, an apostle of Christ Jesus by the will of God, and Timothy our brother,

To the church of God that is in Corinth, including all the saints throughout Achaia:

Grace to you and peace from God our Father and the Lord Jesus Christ. (2 Cor. 1:1–2)

Paul an apostle—sent neither by human commission nor from human authorities, but through Jesus Christ and God the Father, who raised him from the dead—and all the members of God's family who are with me,

To the churches of Galatia:

Grace to you and peace from God our Father and the Lord Jesus Christ, who gave himself for our sins to set us free from the present evil age, according to the will of our God and Father, to whom be the glory forever and ever. Amen. (Gal. 1:1–5)

Paul, an apostle of Christ Jesus by the will of God,

To the saints who are in Ephesus and are faithful in Christ Jesus:

Grace to you and peace from God our Father and the Lord Jesus Christ. (Eph. 1:1–2)

Paul and Timothy, servants of Christ Jesus,

To all the saints in Christ Jesus who are in Philippi, with the bishops and deacons:

Grace to you and peace from God our Father and the Lord Jesus Christ. (Phil. 1:1–2)

Paul, an apostle of Christ Jesus by the will of God, and Timothy our brother,

To the saints and faithful brothers and sisters in Christ in Colossae:

Grace to you and peace from God our Father. (Col. 1:1–2)

Paul, Silvanus, and Timothy,

To the church of the Thessalonians in God the Father and the Lord Jesus Christ:

Grace to you and peace. (1 Thess. 1:1)

Paul, Silvanus, and Timothy,

To the church of the Thessalonians in God our Father and the Lord Jesus Christ:

Grace to you and peace from God our Father and the Lord Jesus Christ. (2 Thess. 1:1–2)

Paul, an apostle of Christ Jesus by the command of God our Savior and of Christ Jesus our hope,
    To Timothy, my loyal child in the faith:
    Grace, mercy, and peace from God the Father and Christ Jesus our Lord. (1 Tim. 1:1–2)

Paul, an apostle of Christ Jesus by the will of God, for the sake of the promise of life that is in Christ Jesus,
    To Timothy, my beloved child:
    Grace, mercy, and peace from God the Father and Christ Jesus our Lord. (2 Tim. 1:1–2)

Paul, a servant of God and an apostle of Jesus Christ, for the sake of the faith of God's elect and the knowledge of the truth that is in accordance with godliness, in the hope of eternal life that God, who never lies, promised before the ages began—in due time he revealed his word through the proclamation with which I have been entrusted by the command of God our Savior,
    To Titus, my loyal child in the faith we share:
    Grace and peace from God the Father and Christ Jesus our Savior. (Titus 1:1–4)

Paul, a prisoner of Christ Jesus, and Timothy our brother,
    To Philemon our dear friend and co-worker, to Apphia our sister, to Archippus our fellow soldier, and to the church in your house:
    Grace to you and peace from God our Father and the Lord Jesus Christ. (Philem. 1–3)

A number of elements are worthy of notice. Paul diverges from common practice by replacing the *chairein* greeting with a "grace" (*charis*) and "peace" (*eirēnē*) greeting. These greetings mention Jesus in all but two of the letters. A coauthor or cosender is mentioned in many cases. Paul frequently refers to his status as an apostle as well.

The differences furnish more clues about Paul's mindset as he addresses his audience. From the outset of Galatians, for example, Paul presses the point that his apostleship is perfectly valid despite the aspersions his opponents have cast on it. The inclusion of Apphia, Archippus, and the church at his house makes clear that the Letter to Philemon is not a letter to Philemon alone and that others will thus be aware of the request Paul has made of him. Romans and Titus feature extremely long prescripts that offer a sort of capsule of Paul's theology. It may be that he feels a need to frame his message since his familiarity with the churches he addresses (in Rome) or discusses (in Crete) is limited.

Nonbiblical letters ordinarily follow the prescript with a health wish. This health wish may take the form of a prayer to the gods (Oxyrhynchus Papyrus 528: "Before all else I pray for your health, and every day and evening I make supplication on your behalf before Thoeris who loves you"), or it may be much simpler (Paris Papyrus 43: "If you are well, it would be excellent; I myself am well").[4] In the New Testament, only 3 John contains a standard health wish: "Beloved, I pray that all may go well with you and that you may be in good health, just as it is well with your soul" (2). Paul's letters lack a health wish, though the thanksgiving found in most of his letters performs a similar function, albeit with a greater emphasis on the spiritual welfare of the recipients than on their physical well-being.

After the prescript comes the thanksgiving, which offers an even better preview of the themes and concerns Paul will discuss in a letter. Since this component is found less frequently in Hellenistic letters than any other element in the opening section, Paul's regular use of the thanksgiving merits attention.

"I give thanks," Paul tells the Corinthians, "because of the grace of God that has been given you in Christ Jesus, for in every way you have been enriched in him, in speech and knowledge of every kind . . . so that you are not lacking in any spiritual gift as you wait for the revealing of our Lord Jesus Christ" (1 Cor. 1:4–7). Here one sees Paul

4. In Latin letters, the most widely used formula was "if you are well, it is well; I also am well" (*si vales, bene est, ego valeo*). The Latin phrase was so common that writers often used the abbreviation SVBEEV instead of spelling it out, in the same way that one might see BTW ("by the way") or FWIW ("for what it's worth") in modern emails and text messages (Hans-Josef Klauck, *Ancient Letters and the New Testament: A Guide to Context and Exegesis* [Waco: Baylor University Press, 2006], 21).

introducing topics that will arise later in his response to their letter to him. Many of their questions deal with the proper disposition of various spiritual gifts (12:1–10), including prophecy (11:2–16) and speaking in tongues (1 Cor. 14). His mention of "knowledge" (*gnōsis*) anticipates the discussion in 1 Cor. 8 about the knowledge that the Corinthians possess and how it can create divisions if not used in the proper spirit. The analysis of the resurrection in 1 Cor. 15 develops the theme of the "revealing" of Jesus (1:7) as well.

Other letters offer similar previews. Paul's thanksgiving in Phil. 1:3–11 refers to their "sharing" (*koinōnia*), the first of several occurrences of this critical motif in a letter expressing gratitude for the readers' generosity and solidarity (2:1; 3:10; 4:15). He thanks the Thessalonians (1 Thess. 1:2–4) for their "work of faith and labor of love and steadfastness of hope," virtues he will list again later (3:6; 4:9). More than anything, they are in danger of losing hope due to the death of community members and perhaps some misunderstanding of Paul's teaching about the end times. That Paul thanks them two more times (2:13; 3:9) is a function of his desire to encourage them and reaffirm them in their fledgling faith. In so short a letter as Philemon, it is likely no accident to find so much language in the thanksgiving appearing elsewhere in the letter, such as kinship terms (1, 2, 3, 7, 10, 16), "love" (5, 7, 9), "heart" (7, 12, 20), and references to imprisonment (1, 9, 10, 13).

Only a few of Paul's letters lack a thanksgiving, and interpreting its absence is a bit tricky. Relations with his audience are strained when he writes 2 Corinthians, which may explain why he just barely manages to slip in a thanksgiving in 1:11—and even then Paul is not the one giving thanks. Similarly tense is his relationship with the Galatians. He moves directly from the salutation and peace wish into the body of his letter, a sharply worded attack on deviant teachings and the lack of fidelity he perceives on the part of the Galatians. Skipping the thanksgiving is Paul's way of expressing his disappointment when he does not feel particularly thankful. But the absence of a thanksgiving in 1 Timothy and Titus, where relations between author and audience are cordial, underscores the limitations of such arguments from silence. Insofar as the thanksgiving was hardly an obligatory element of Greco-Roman letters, its absence would not necessarily have been as jarring as modern scholars often assume.[5] Would Paul have expected the Galatians to get such a message? Would they have noticed something missing if they were unaware of his standard practice? Neither question has an obvious answer.

Ending a Letter

Small touches at the end of a letter can likewise be pregnant with significance. During the Revolutionary War, Abigail Adams concluded many of her letters to her husband by signing "Portia." John Adams never reciprocated by signing the name of Portia's husband, "Brutus," the Roman senator who participated in the assassination of Julius Caesar. Perhaps it made him nervous to ponder how quickly those who oppose tyrants can meet their demise.

Instead of a signature, Hellenistic letters typically conclude with a simple farewell (usually with the word *errōso* or *errōsthe*) and a wish for the good health and welfare of the addressee(s). Paul makes certain modifications to this pattern. Pauline letters generally conclude with (1) peace wish, (2) greetings, and (3) benediction.

The peace wish shows the influence of Jewish custom on Paul's letter-writing habits. Jewish letters use the word *shalom*, which becomes *eirēnē* when Paul is writing in Greek. He includes the peace even when writing a non-Jewish audience like the Thessalonians (2 Thess. 3:16: "Now may the Lord of peace himself give you peace at all times and in all ways"). This element, however, is the least consistent. Of the thirteen letters, six lack a peace wish (1 Corinthians, Colossians, 1–2 Timothy, Titus, Philemon).

Greetings appear in nine of the thirteen letters. Paul himself sends greetings to groups or individuals on the receiving end or relays greetings from those who are with him where he is writing. In some cases he urges them to "greet one another with a holy kiss" (Romans, 1–2 Corinthians, 1 Thessalonians). Usually these greetings are brief: "Greet every saint in Christ Jesus. The friends who are with me greet you.

---

5. Robert Van Voorst, "Why Is There No Thanksgiving Period in Galatians? An Assessment of an Exegetical Commonplace," *Journal of Biblical Literature* 129 (2010): 153–72.

All the saints greet you, especially those of the emperor's household"
(Phil. 4:21–22); or: "All who are with me send greetings to you. Greet
those who love us in the faith" (Titus 3:15). Romans stands out from
the other letters as Paul greets more than two dozen named individuals and a handful of specific groups, some of whom he has met and
others he has not. These greetings contain valuable information about
the circumstances in which Paul finds himself, the extensive network
of followers and coworkers with whom he is engaged in ministry, and
the audience he is addressing. The absence of greetings in Ephesians
is probably due to its origins as a circular letter intended for multiple
audiences not known to one another. Scholars suggest that the absent
greetings in Galatians and 2 Thessalonians may be a function of the
urgency of the occasion, but it would not be at all unprecedented for
an author to end a letter abruptly.

In place of the Hellenistic farewell wish, Paul ends all of his New
Testament letters with a benediction. The form features only minor
variations. Second Thessalonians 3:18 is representative: "The grace
of our Lord Jesus Christ be with all of you." The inclusion of Jesus
in the benediction is a sign of how quickly and profoundly Paul's
conversion influenced even so mundane a habit as concluding a letter.

An additional element seen near the end of five letters is a sign that
Paul is writing in his own hand (1 Cor. 16:21; Gal. 6:11; Col. 4:18;
2 Thess. 3:17; Philem. 19). Since we do not possess the autographs
(the original handwritten manuscripts), it is unclear whether Paul is
indicating that he has written the entire letter himself or is only signing it in his own hand after dictating most of it to a scribe. Neither
practice would have been out of the ordinary.

The Body

However revealing the opening and conclusion may be, the body contains the main substance of a letter. The opening may foreshadow
what comes in the body, and the closing may echo it or look forward
to a time when Paul can speak to his audience face to face, but what
stands in between is the subject prompting him to write in the first
place. Close examination of his letters reveals that Paul has not thrown

them together haphazardly. They are structured so that *how* he says something does not detract from *what* he wants to say.

Apart from its length, the body of 1 Corinthians most closely resembles a modern letter. The Corinthians have written to Paul with a number of questions. Roughly half of 1 Corinthians consists of his responses, from the beginning of 1 Cor. 7 ("now concerning the matters about which you wrote") to the end of 1 Cor. 14. Earlier sections of the body touch on matters about which Paul has heard through mutual acquaintances (1:11; 5:1). Other passages introduce new topics that are related to the issues raised by their questions. Although certain passages display an internal structure or logic, the letter as a whole is organized in a very loose fashion.

Point-by-point responses to specific queries as one finds in 1 Corinthians, however, is not the structural norm for Paul's letters. Alternating between exposition and exhortation is the more common argumentative pattern.

Exposition and Exhortation

Exposition refers to the process of imparting information or explaining something that is difficult to understand. Expository writing provides background and sets out the meaning of a text. Grammatically speaking, it takes the indicative mood. Pauline exposition often focuses on texts from the Hebrew Bible and involves description, analysis, and commentary.[6] Examples of extended exposition in the letters are plentiful. In Romans, he describes the depraved state of all humanity (1:18–32); the equal accountability of all, Jew and gentile alike, before the judgment seat (Rom. 2); the justification available through faith (3:21–31; cf. Gal. 3:6–28); the example of Abraham in the history of God's dealings with humanity (Rom. 4); and the relationship of Jews and gentiles in salvation history (Rom. 9–11; cf. Eph. 2:11–22). In 2 Corinthians, he compares and contrasts the old and new covenants (3:1–4:6; cf. Gal. 4:21–5:1) and delineates his role as a minister of the new (2 Cor. 4:7–5:10). Every letter contains instances of briefer exposition that form the basis for subsequent exhortation.

6. For discussion of Paul's way of reading and interpreting the Old Testament, see chapter 5.

If exposition occurs in the indicative mood, exhortation occurs in the imperative. To exhort can mean to urge, warn, advise, encourage, coax, rouse, cajole, motivate, provoke, embolden, induce, command, or inspire. Hortatory writing or speech elicits a response from the audience; it calls for a specific way of acting or thinking. Three main modes of exhortation are seen in the writings of the popular philosophers who, like Paul, sought to influence the beliefs and behaviors of their audiences: (1) protrepsis, (2) parenesis, and (3) diatribe.[7]

Protreptic discourse is designed to recruit or win adherents to a particular way of life. It often seeks to persuade students to adopt a lifestyle devoted to philosophy as opposed to the more practical fields of oratory or politics. Much of the protreptic literature from antiquity is produced by a particular philosophical school whose members seek to distinguish their system from that of rival schools. Stoics and Epicureans not only tout the advantages of their respective approaches to the good life, but they also expose what they regard as the inconsistency and ill effects of the alternative. Second-century Christians such as Justin Martyr and Clement of Alexandria produce protreptic works, but the readers of Paul's letters have already embraced the new life to which he invites his audiences as he travels around the Mediterranean. Although portions of Romans, for example, may echo arguments he makes when facing pagan (1:18–2:11) or Jewish (2:12–4:25) audiences, in his letters he is preaching to the choir.

Parenesis seeks to influence behavior, either by persuasion or dissuasion. Originality is not the aim of parenetic discourse. When Paul urges the Philippians to dwell on "whatever is true, . . . honorable, . . . just, . . . pure, . . . pleasing, . . . commendable," and so forth (4:8), he is not trying to impress them with a novel idea. Nor is he teaching the Thessalonians anything new when he advises them to "abstain from every form of evil" (1 Thess. 5:22). If such basic ethical insights are alien to his audience, Paul truly has his work cut out for him. Rather than present new ideas, Hellenistic writers engaged in parenesis want their readers to carry on with what they already know to be good and true. This approach is seen in Paul's frequent use of the phrase "as

7. Abraham J. Malherbe, *Moral Exhortation: A Greco-Roman Sourcebook*, Library of Early Christianity 4 (Philadelphia: Westminster, 1986), 121–34.

you know" (1 Thess. 2:11; 3:4) and reminders of their past experience (Phil. 3:1; 1 Thess. 2:9; 2 Thess. 3:7).

Not only is such moral instruction not new to his readers, but by and large it is also not particularly unique to Christianity. Its content is traditional in nature. Parallels to the specific advice Paul dispenses can be found throughout the works of Jewish and Greco-Roman writers who made use of many of the same *topoi*, stock arguments on ethical subjects that might feature common clichés, sayings, or definitions.[8] For example, Paul's discussions of government authority (Rom. 13:1–7; Titus 3:1–2), community and individuality (1 Cor. 12:12–27), idleness (2 Thess. 3:6–13), and anger management (Eph. 4:31–32) are grounded in his Christian worldview, but they echo many of the same arguments one might find in Cicero, Dio Chrysostom, or Plutarch.

Similarities to non-Christian literature are also plentiful in terms of social setting and parenetic method. The one receiving advice is in a personal relationship with and subordinate to the one giving it. That Paul's letters have this parenetic character reveals something about the nature of the bond he has formed with his readers. Expressions of confidence in the letters are consistent with what one would expect when a social superior offers encouragement to a protégé (2 Cor. 7:4, 16; Gal. 5:10; 2 Thess. 3:4). Paul's presentation of himself as an example for his readers to emulate is unremarkable in this light (1 Cor. 4:16; 11:1; 2 Thess. 3:7–10). Even where there was not a close relationship, the use of concrete examples could move an audience more effectively than the most articulate analyses of virtue and vice (Gal. 3:6–10; Phil. 2:19–30; 2 Tim. 1:5).

In modern parlance, a diatribe is an angry speech denouncing someone or something. Diatribe in ancient Greece and Rome is instead a genre or style of discussion and debate widely used in philosophical schools.[9] The subject is often a question of ethical theory or practice. The aim is to persuade an audience by anticipating and removing any obstacles or objections to the speaker's position on the subject under discussion. Characteristic of the diatribe is its dialogical nature. The

8. Ibid., 144–45.
9. Stanley K. Stowers, "Diatribe," in *The Anchor Bible Dictionary*, ed. D. N. Freedman et al. (New York: Doubleday, 1992), 2:190–93.

speaker voices and then addresses the hypothetical questions and faulty conclusions of an imaginary interlocutor ("some might say . . ."). Even in written form, the diatribe simulates the Socratic, back-and-forth exchange between teachers and students or between opponents in a debate.

Paul adapts the diatribe to his letters, most conspicuously in Romans but also to a degree in 1 Corinthians. In Romans he argues that, when compared with the gentiles, the relationship of the Jews with their Creator is impaired as a result of sin. Given their status as the chosen people, Paul recognizes a reasonable question that might arise: "Then what advantage has the Jew? Or what is the value of circumcision?" (3:1). His response: "Much, in every way. For in the first place the Jews were entrusted with the oracles of God" (3:2). At this and many other points, he pauses to ask a rhetorical question that expresses an objection that he has heard previously or expects to hear: "Did what is good, then, bring death to me?" (7:13); "I ask, then, has God rejected his people?" (11:1); "Have they stumbled so as to fall?" (11:11). The question from the imaginary interlocutor is an attempt to refute Paul's position by exposing it as absurd. If divine grace is the response to human sin, "Should we continue in sin in order that grace may abound?" (6:1). Paul's "reply" is a consistent "By no means!" after which he proceeds to clear away the fallacious reasoning that underlies the objection.

The rhetorical questions in 1 Corinthians often represent Paul's own attempt to highlight the incoherence of the thinking or behavior he opposes: "Do you not know that you are God's temple and that God's Spirit dwells in you?" (3:16); "Do you not know that wrongdoers will not inherit the kingdom of God?" (6:9); "Do you not know that your bodies are members of Christ?" (6:15). Here and elsewhere he assumes that his audience already agrees with him on the basic principle at stake but have temporarily forgotten it or swerved inadvertently from the truth, as when he wonders, "Now if Christ is proclaimed as raised from the dead, how can some of you say there is no resurrection of the dead?" (15:12).[10]

10. The Corinthians apparently accept the claim that Christ rose from the dead on Easter, but some are denying that there will be a general resurrection of all the faithful at the end of time. Their otherwise undocumented practice of vicarious baptism "on behalf of the dead," according to Paul, is futile if the dead have no hope of rising (1 Cor. 15:29).

Due to the state of the ancient manuscripts, following this dialogical give-and-take is not always as straightforward as one might hope. Like most documents, Paul's letters lacked punctuation. Navigating any text without the aid of punctuation can be a challenge. Several examples of this phenomenon occur in 1 Corinthians. Some critics label Paul a prude on the basis of 7:1, where he writes, "It is well for a man not to touch a woman." Without quotation marks, this phrase certainly leaves the impression that Paul holds a negative view of sexuality. But if, as commentators generally agree, this is a statement to which he is responding, Paul's stance looks very different. His subsequent treatment of sex and marriage in 1 Cor. 7 makes it fairly clear that the sentiment in the opening verse is not exactly his own, just as the context of Col. 2:21 ("Do not handle, Do not taste, Do not touch") helps the reader recognize that Paul is quoting someone advocating extreme asceticism and not speaking for himself. Unfortunately, it is not always so easy, especially when Paul quotes a slogan and then modifies or undercuts it in the very next line.[11]

The arrangement of the exhortation (protrepsis, parenesis, and diatribe) in relation to the exposition varies from letter to letter. In a few letters, the bulk of the exposition and exhortation are grouped together in separate sections. The transition in Romans comes at the beginning of Rom. 12 ("I appeal to you therefore . . . to present your bodies as a living sacrifice, holy and acceptable to God") after eleven chapters of dense exposition. In Galatians, Paul builds a case for his understanding of the gospel on Scripture and experience before spelling out the ethical corollary in 5:1–6:10: "For freedom Christ has set us free. Stand firm, therefore, and do not submit again to a yoke of slavery." The "indicative" about what God has wrought falls in the first half of Ephesians (1:3–3:21) while the "imperative" about how to walk as children of the light falls in the second half (4:1–6:20).

It is more common to find exposition and exhortation interspersed throughout a letter, one following fast upon the other and connected

11. Examples punctuated according to the NRSV include "'All things are lawful for me,' but not all things are beneficial" (1 Cor. 6:12); "'Food is meant for the stomach and the stomach for food,' and God will destroy both one and the other" (6:13); "We know that 'all of us possess knowledge.' Knowledge puffs up, but love builds up" (8:1).

James versus Paul?

Paul is not the only New Testament author to use the diatribe style. The Letter of James also uses it in its oft-cited argument that "faith without works is . . . dead" (2:18–26). When the author remarks that "a person is justified by works and not by faith alone" (2:24), he seems to be addressing the same theme as Paul in Romans and Galatians. Many scholars believe that Paul himself is the unnamed opponent the author has in mind in James 2:18 ("but someone will say . . .") and that his aim is to counter the popularity of Paul's doctrine of justification by faith. Some believe that James (or a person writing in his name) misunderstands Paul's position, while others, like Martin Luther, believe that James understands him all too well but rejects the radical implications of his argument. Still others hold that James and Paul are not addressing one another at all but, rather, are independently adding their voices to a debate taking place within first-century Judaism.

---

by a conjunction such as "for" or "therefore." Thus Paul tells the Philippians, "Work out your own salvation with fear and trembling; for it is God who is at work in you, enabling you both to will and to work for his good pleasure" (2:12–13). "Therefore encourage one another," he instructs the Thessalonians, because God has destined them not for wrath but for salvation (1 Thess. 5:9–11). The command that women should "learn in silence with full submission" in 1 Tim. 2:11 is issued on biblical grounds: "For Adam was formed first, then Eve; and Adam was not deceived, but the woman was deceived and became a transgressor" (2:13–14). The joining of "is" (what Paul asserts or argues to be true) with "ought" (what Paul says should happen) occurs so frequently that it is possible to overlook it. But one of the best strategies for thinking Paul's thoughts after him is to pay close attention when he gives explicit rationales for the specific actions and attitudes he is advocating, especially when he makes statements that are odd, confusing, or even repugnant to contemporary sensibilities.

Paul and Ancient Rhetoric

The study of ancient rhetoric has inspired more elaborate, detailed attempts at analyzing Paul's arguments as they unfold in the body of a letter. Rhetoric, like diatribe, carries a pejorative connotation today.

Lawyers and politicians engage in rhetoric—for many, this alone is ample evidence of an intent to mislead or manipulate. Hostility to rhetoric goes back to the ancient world, however, when writers like Plato bemoaned the ability of Sophists like Protagoras "to make the weaker argument appear the stronger." This charge was also among those for which his teacher Socrates was tried and executed (*Apologia* 19b).

To be sure, rhetoric can be used for undesirable purposes, but its reputation for deceptiveness is not entirely fair. Strictly speaking, rhetoric is the art of effective communication. It played an important part in education in Greece and Rome, where its primary purpose was to train future leaders to speak persuasively. Over the centuries the art of rhetoric was reduced to a system through which anyone—and not just those with the natural gift of eloquence—could potentially master the basics of public speaking. Among the most influential rhetorical guides were works by Aristotle, Cicero, Quintilian, and the anonymous author of *Rhetorica ad Herennium*. Although few may stop to think of it, anyone who seeks to persuade or influence by means of language is practicing rhetoric. Paul certainly falls in this group, whether or not he has read any of the classic texts.

Ancient theorists recognized three species of rhetoric: judicial/forensic, epideictic/demonstrative, and deliberative. The aim of judicial or forensic rhetoric is to convince an audience of the guilt or innocence of a person or group standing accused of particular actions in the past. It is naturally found in legal settings. The *Apology* of Socrates is a classic (if unsuccessful) example. The aim of epideictic rhetoric is to celebrate or denigrate certain ideas, virtues, or individuals. The setting is typically a ceremonial occasion such as a funeral. Lincoln's Gettysburg Address and Martin Luther King Jr.'s "I Have a Dream" speech are often cited as examples of epideictic rhetoric. The aim of deliberative rhetoric is to persuade an audience to pursue or avoid a certain course of action in the future. While it is most closely associated with political speech, deliberative rhetoric is found whenever an audience is asked to decide which of two deeds or policies is the more honorable, ethical, or advantageous. Patrick Henry's "Liberty or Death" speech and portions of the Sermon on the Mount fit the description of deliberative rhetoric.

These three types of rhetoric feature three types of arguments: appeals to *ethos*, *pathos*, and *logos* (Aristotle, *Rhetorica* 1356a). *Ethos* arguments draw support from the character of the speaker. If an audience views the source of an argument as credible and trustworthy, they are more likely to find the argument persuasive. Makers of television advertisements understand this principle well. Commercials for aspirin and toothpaste include doctors and dentists. Sympathetic celebrities make better salesmen than those tainted by scandal. Candidates for public office never ask disgraced politicians for official endorsements. *Pathos* arguments play on the emotions of the audience. Joy, fear, anger, guilt, and pity are powerful motivations, provided the speaker can successfully arouse them in the audience. Jonathan Edwards's 1741 "Sinners in the Hands of an Angry God" sermon is a famous example of the appeal to *pathos*. *Logos* arguments rely primarily on reason for their persuasive force. They make greater use of facts, analogies, and examples and pay closer attention to premises, cause and effect, and supporting evidence. An appeal to *logos* may follow the rough outline of a deductive syllogism, but it may also take different forms, such as satire (Jonathan Swift's "A Modest Proposal").

Individual speeches ideally contain four main parts according to ancient rhetoricians:

1. The *exordium* serves as an introduction.
2. The *narratio* provides the essential facts and basic background of the subject at hand. This section often includes a *propositio*, a concise statement of the position or thesis for which the speaker will argue in the following section.
3. The *probatio*, sometimes called the *argumentatio* or the *confirmatio*, constitutes the main body. Here one finds the argument for or proof of the author's main point.
4. In the *peroratio*, the speaker concludes by summarizing the main points and making a final pitch for the sympathy of the audience.

To what extent do these considerations shed light on Paul's letters? It depends in part on the answer to another question, namely, is a letter a letter or is it a speech? Rhetoric in the ancient world applied to speeches, not to letters. In Paul's case, the distinction is not so cut-and-dried because he is writing true letters responding to specific situations, yet he expects them to be delivered orally to an assembled audience; in other words, since the setting in which the letter is received or read is very much like the setting of a public speech, it is possible that Paul composed his letters with the corresponding rhetorical conventions in mind. On this score, many of his letters are like other early Christian writings, such as Hebrews and 1 John.

That Paul makes use of the three modes of persuasion is obvious. Autobiographical statements scattered throughout the letters (e.g., 2 Cor. 1:8–2:13; 10:7–12:18; Gal. 1:13–2:14; Phil. 1:12–26; 3:2–14; 1 Thess. 2:1–12; 2 Tim. 3:10–13) establish his character, thereby bolstering his arguments by reminding his readers that—should they be inclined to question him—he deserves the benefit of the doubt. The emotional texture of his letters is likewise palpable. *Pathos* arguments appear regularly. He evokes fear when he informs the Corinthians that their improper behavior at the Lord's Supper has resulted in the illness and even the death of some of their members (1 Cor. 11:27–30). Earlier in the letter he tells them, "I am not writing this to make you ashamed, but to admonish you as my beloved children" (4:14). Any parent or child will immediately recognize such a remark as intended to administer, if not shame, at least a healthy dose of guilt. When he compliments the Thessalonians for their exemplary faith and love (1 Thess. 1:2–3; 3:6; 4:9–10), he wants to produce feelings of confidence. Finally, Paul makes abundant use of *logos* arguments. He arrives at the idea of "justification by faith" in Gal. 3:6–18 through his interpretation of Gen. 15:6 ("and he *believed* the LORD; and the LORD reckoned it to him as *righteousness*" [emphasis added]), reasoning that Abraham could not have been made righteous by obeying the law since Moses received the law centuries after Abraham was dead. He cites the testimony of over five hundred witnesses to argue for the historicity of the bodily resurrection of Jesus (1 Cor. 15:3–8) and spends the rest of the chapter extrapolating from this to a larger point about the fate of the body and soul of all believers. Analogies from the realms of family (Gal. 3:23–4:7), anatomy (1 Cor. 12:12–26), animal husbandry (1 Cor. 9:8–9; 1 Tim. 5:17–18), botany (Rom. 11:17–24), and especially history as related in Scripture (Rom. 9:10–18, 27–33;

11:7–12; 1 Cor. 10:1–13; Gal. 4:21–31) help Paul to explain key ethical and theological principles and demonstrate their plausibility.

It is also evident that Paul engages in the three different species of rhetoric recognized by Greco-Roman theorists. Portions of 2 Corinthians (2 Cor. 1–7 and 10–13) and Galatians (Gal. 1–2) closely resemble forensic rhetoric, even if the precise charges against which Paul is defending himself are difficult to reconstruct. Romans and 1 Thessalonians have been described as pieces of epideictic rhetoric insofar as Paul affirms values he shares in common with his readers. The "hymn to love" in 1 Cor. 13 has also been placed in this category. The vast majority of Paul's letters are deliberative in nature, seeking to persuade his readers to pursue a course of action or to dissuade them from another. This also includes sections of letters such as Romans and 2 Corinthians that operate for significant stretches along the lines of forensic and epideictic oratory. Paul is attempting to affect some change in the thinking or acting of his audience. Although it is impossible to place each letter in its entirety into a single category, it is wise to keep these three types of rhetoric in mind in order to avoid reading too much or too little into particular literary features. For example, Paul's curious linguistic and historical observations in Gal. 3–4 are more compelling when they are seen primarily as part of a rhetorical strategy to combat a certain form of legalism rather than as an attempt to prove certain facts.[12]

Somewhat less certain is the degree to which the structure of Paul's letters conforms to the standard divisions of forensic and deliberative speeches. It is not that there is any shortage of attempts to analyze the letters rhetorically. Since the seminal work of Hans Dieter Betz on Galatians, a small cottage industry has sprung up devoted to rhetorical analysis of the letters.[13] Betz regards Galatians as an example of forensic rhetoric designed to rebut the accusations of the Judaizers and generates a detailed outline of the argument: epistolary prescript (1:1–5), *exordium* (1:6–11), *narratio* (1:12–2:14), *propositio* (2:15–21), *probatio* (3:1–4:31), *exhortatio* (5:1–6:10), and *conclusio*

---

12. Cf. Steven L. McKenzie, *How to Read the Bible* (Oxford: Oxford University Press, 2005), 164.

13. H. D. Betz, *Galatians: A Commentary on Paul's Letter to the Churches in Galatia*, Hermeneia (Philadelphia: Fortress, 1979).

(6:11–18). But other scholars, building on Betz's analysis, make different divisions. The *confirmatio*, for example, has been identified in at least five different blocks (1:10–6:10; 3:1–4:11; 1:11–5:1; 3:6–4:7; and 2:15–6:17), and the *propositio* with at least three different blocks (1:6–9; 2:14–21; and 2:14–3:5).[14] Which analysis—if any—is correct? One sometimes has the impression that Paul's interpreters have spent far more time and effort thinking about the precise organization of the letters than Paul has himself. As a general rule, the more intricate the structural analysis, the more tentative and precarious are the interpretations that rely on it. It is undeniable that many of the letters follow Greco-Roman rhetorical patterns. It is likewise undeniable that some do not follow such patterns in any appreciable way and that insisting on observing them is the equivalent of forcing square pegs into round holes.

Conclusion

Not all ways of saying what one wants to say are equally effective, as anyone who has been misunderstood will readily attest. Paul certainly learned this lesson. Responding to a reported case of incest in Corinth, he says, "I wrote to you in my letter not to associate with sexually immoral persons" (1 Cor. 5:9). By this, he continues, he did not mean "the immoral of this world, or the greedy and robbers, or idolaters." If this had been his meaning, then they would "need to go out of the world" since it is patently impossible to avoid all contact with sinners in a world where everyone is a sinner. Paul meant something different: "But now I am writing to you not to associate with anyone *who bears the name of brother or sister* who is sexually immoral or greedy, or is an idolater, reviler, drunkard, or robber" (5:11, emphasis added).[15] Communal discipline is his concern, not isolation from the population outside the group. Either he said something other than what he meant to say or his readers were not paying sufficient attention.

14. See the charts in Jerome Murphy-O'Connor, *Paul the Letter-Writer: His World, His Options, His Skills* (Collegeville, MN: Michael Glazier/Liturgical Press, 1995), 77–79.

15. The Revised Standard Version ("but rather I wrote to you . . .") is equally valid for the ambiguous tense of the Greek verb in 5:11.

Were it not for such interjections, it might be easy to forget that Paul occasionally failed to connect with his readers on the first try. Paul wrote letters out of necessity. It was not his preferred method for communicating with the churches he had founded or with his coworkers in the missionary field. Personal meetings offered the opportunity to clear up potential misunderstandings with his readers rather than waiting weeks or months, only to discover the confusion long after it had done damage to the relationship. For this reason, Paul's oft-stated desire to visit his readers is more than a mere literary device (Rom. 1:11; 1 Thess. 2:17–18; 2 Tim. 1:4; 4:9, 21; Philem. 22).

Notwithstanding periodic miscommunications and Paul's self-deprecating comments about his meager abilities as a speaker (cf. 1 Cor. 2:1), the popularity and influence of his letters over the centuries are a testimony to his considerable rhetorical skill. This is not to suggest that he had studied Isocrates or Aristotle or Cicero. Neither Barack Obama nor Ronald Reagan had much, if any, formal training in rhetoric in their student days, yet many consider both to be masterful communicators. (Their speechwriters, of course, may be a different story.) But even if Paul had received such training, it might be hard to tell. According to the principle of *dissimulatio artis*, effective orators make sure to conceal their knowledge of rhetorical theory, especially when they are seeking to gain the audience's goodwill (*Rhetorica ad Herennium* 4.7.10; cf. Aristotle, *Rhetorica* 1404b). Like many pastors and politicians, however, it is safe to assume that Paul had acquired an informal education in rhetoric if only through frequent exposure to more seasoned orators.

Scholars now and then go overboard in their "discovery" of elaborate rhetorical or structural patterns that purportedly hold the key to unlocking Paul's arguments. If the flow of a letter fails to correspond to what one would expect from studying ancient rhetoric, some scholars then argue that its present form is not what Paul actually composed. In this approach, the natural conclusion is that someone must have stitched together fragments or whole letters that did not originally belong together. This approach is seen most often with 2 Corinthians and Philippians. But the reasoning that underlies it is circular. It is obvious that a "disruptive" passage in a letter is the result of a textual interpolation only if one already assumes that Paul adheres to the

---

Non-Pauline Interpolations

An interpolation is a word, phrase, sentence, or paragraph that has been intentionally or unintentionally inserted into a text. In biblical studies, it usually refers to an insertion into the original manuscript by a later scribe during the copying process. Scholars have identified a number of passages in Paul's letters that they believe may have been inserted by someone other than Paul:

Rom. 16:25–27	Gal. 2:7–8
1 Cor. 11:3–16	Phil. 1:1c
1 Cor. 14:33b–36	1 Thess. 2:14–16
2 Cor. 6:14–7:1	

Although the argument for some of these passages being interpolations (e.g., Rom. 16:25–27) is stronger than for others, scholarly debate continues for each case.

---

rules of ancient rhetoric as a standard practice, which is precisely the question that has yet to receive a definitive answer. Analyzing Paul's letters would be much easier if interpreters knew which set of literary guidelines he followed, but epistolary and rhetorical practice do not always match theory. Persuasion of the sort one sees in the letters is an art, not a science. Quintilian, himself one of the foremost ancient authorities on whom modern scholars rely for their rhetorical analyses, gives a good reason to be wary of the overzealous application of rhetorical categories to Paul's writings when he notes that letters only rarely follow a rigid organizational scheme (*Institutio oratoria* 9.4.19–20).[16]

Reading Paul's letters through the lens of rhetoric nevertheless has the great merit of focusing close attention on what he is trying to accomplish by writing. Paul is not writing simply to keep in touch with his friends and followers. He has something specific to say and wants his audience to respond appropriately. Many ancient methods of argumentation are still common today, though some may be peculiar to Paul's context. Knowing how Paul's contemporaries sought

---

16. Exceptions to this rule are sometimes found, Quintilian says, when a letter deals with "philosophy, politics, or the like." Might Paul's letters qualify as such an exception?

to persuade their audiences makes it easier to understand his teachings and follow his train of thought, even when it moves in an unexpected direction.

For Further Discussion

1. In terms of form, what are the differences and similarities between ancient and modern letters?
2. How does Paul conform to and deviate from the standard practices in ancient Greece and Rome for organizing a letter?
3. Which of the three species of ancient rhetoric (judicial/forensic, epideictic/demonstrative, deliberative) appears most often in Paul's writings? Does Paul tend to make appeals and arguments on the basis of *ethos*, *pathos*, or *logos*?

For Further Reading

Anderson, R. D., Jr. *Ancient Rhetorical Theory and Paul*. Rev. ed. Leuven: Peeters, 1999.

Arzt, P. "The 'Epistolary Introductory Thanksgiving' in the Papyri and Paul." *Novum Testamentum* 36 (1994): 29–46.

Bahr, G. J. "Paul and Letter Writing in the First Century." *Catholic Biblical Quarterly* 28 (1966): 465–77.

Classen, C. J. "St. Paul's Epistles and Ancient Greek and Roman Rhetoric." In *Rhetoric and the New Testament: Essays from the 1992 Heidelberg Conference*, edited by S. E. Porter and T. H. Olbricht, 265–91. Sheffield: Sheffield Academic Press, 1993.

Forbes, Christopher. "Comparison, Self-Praise, and Irony: Paul's Boasting and Conventions of Hellenistic Rhetoric." *New Testament Studies* 32 (1986): 1–30.

Harvey, John. *Listening to the Text: Oral Patterning in Paul's Letters*. Grand Rapids: Baker, 1998.

Kennedy, George. *New Testament Interpretation through Rhetorical Criticism*. Chapel Hill: University of North Carolina Press, 1984.

Malherbe, Abraham J. *Moral Exhortation: A Greco-Roman Sourcebook*. Library of Early Christianity 4. Philadelphia: Westminster, 1986.

O'Brien, P. T. *Introductory Thanksgivings in the Letters of Paul*. Novum Testamentum Supplement 49. Leiden: Brill, 1977.

Porter, Stanley E., ed. *Handbook of Classical Rhetoric in the Hellenistic Period, 330 B.C.–A.D. 400.* Leiden: Brill, 1997.

———. "The Theoretical Justification for the Application of Rhetorical Categories to Pauline Epistolary Literature." In *Rhetoric and the New Testament: Essays from the 1992 Heidelberg Conference*, edited by S. E. Porter and T. H. Olbricht, 100–122. Sheffield: Sheffield Academic Press, 1993.

Roetzel, Calvin J. *The Letters of Paul: Conversations in Context.* Atlanta: John Knox, 1982.

Schubert, Paul. *Form and Function of the Pauline Thanksgivings.* Beihefte zur Zeitschrift für die Neutestamentliche Wissenschaft 20. Berlin: Töpelmann, 1939.

Weima, J. A. D. *Neglected Endings: The Significance of the Pauline Letter Closings.* Sheffield: JSOT Press, 1994.

White, John L. *The Form and Function of the Body of the Greek Letter: A Study of the Letter-Body in the Non-literary Papyri and in Paul the Apostle.* Society of Biblical Literature Dissertation Series 2. Missoula, MT: Scholars Press, 1972.

Wilson, Walter T. *Pauline Parallels: A Comprehensive Guide.* Louisville: Westminster John Knox, 2009.

4

✳ *✳* *✳*

Paul's Audiences

Reading Paul's letters today is an exercise in reading over the shoulders of relative strangers. Who were the Romans, the Corinthians, the Galatians, the Ephesians, the Philippians, the Colossians, and the Thessalonians? Who were Timothy, Titus, and Philemon? They were Paul's first readers, who, presumably, had no need for a book on how to read Paul's letters. More accurately, they were his first listeners since most of the letters were addressed to groups rather than to individuals and were likely read aloud at community gatherings (Col. 4:16; 1 Thess. 5:27; cf. Acts 15:30–31). Eavesdropping, then, may be the more apt analogy for reading Paul.

Writers from the Roman period all the way up to the present have made abundant use of eavesdropping as a literary device because of the hijinks that can ensue when one party misconstrues an overheard conversation. Shakespeare constructs the plot of *Much Ado about Nothing* around misunderstood conversations—to considerable comic effect. As Desdemona finds out in *Othello*, however, the results are not always humorous. Even when the identity of the primary participants is certain, making sense of private communication as an outsider is no simple task. When the precise identities are less certain, the risk of misinterpretation is much greater.

Consider, for example, this impudent opening in a letter addressed to Helen Keller: "Allow me to introduce myself. I am a writer and part-time English professor. I am American, married, middle-aged, middle class. Like you, I am blind, though not deaf. But the most important thing you need to know about me, and the reason for my letter, is that I grew up hating you." From this salutation one might surmise that the intended audience is the famous author and speaker whose life is the subject of the 1962 movie *The Miracle Worker*. In fact, the author knows that Keller will never read this letter because she composed it decades after Keller had died.[1] Georgina Kleege wrote this letter as a therapeutic exercise in response to her own frustration with the impossibly high standard of perseverance and cheerfulness set by Keller in the face of adversity. Her one-sided correspondence also provides a forum for reflection on "the idea that disability is a personal tragedy to be overcome through an individual's fortitude and pluck, rather than a set of cultural practices and assumptions."[2] Kleege's true audience is thus very different from and much larger than it at first appears.

Discovering as much information as possible about the intended reader is a wise strategy for interpreting any text. This is especially true for letters. Clues about the identity of the audience actually addressed in a letter can be found even in eccentric examples like Kleege's letters to Helen Keller. In more typical cases, writers rarely need to describe their readers in the body of a letter for the obvious reason that the readers are well aware of who they are. The letters themselves nevertheless contain the best available evidence for sketching a general portrait of Paul's original audiences. Establishing a clearer idea of the reader(s) Paul is addressing is one key to discerning the message he is trying to convey.

Identifying Paul's First Readers

What do Paul's audiences have in common? Each consists of Christians. While his arguments may appeal to nonbelievers as well, they

1. Georgina Kleege, *Blind Rage: Letters to Helen Keller* (Washington, DC: Gallaudet University Press, 2006), 1.
2. Ibid.

are aimed at groups and individuals who have already professed faith in Jesus as Lord. Insofar as each letter shows no sign of having been translated from another language, it is also safe to assume that his readers understand Greek. Beyond this, it is difficult to make blanket statements about Paul's readers. Each audience has its own distinctive profile. Letters for which Paul's authorship is disputed present special challenges when it comes to reconstructing the original audience.[3] What follows are preliminary sketches for the thirteen letters.

Romans

"Rome" and "the church" are virtually synonymous for many modern readers, who see images of St. Peter's Basilica and the ceiling of the Sistine Chapel when they think of the Eternal City. But when Paul writes to "all God's beloved in Rome" (1:7), he is addressing a tiny minority living in the empire's largest city. The Christian community at Rome has no centralized meeting place. They are scattered throughout the city and meet in the homes of individuals such as Prisca and Aquila, Aristobulus, Narcissus, and Philologus (16:3–15). For this reason, Paul's courier (probably Phoebe; 16:1) would have read the letter on multiple occasions for different gatherings.

Without the personal touches found in other letters, Romans has the feel of a theological treatise. This is partly due to Paul's not founding the church there. Paul is not a father figure, unlike the status he enjoys with the Galatians and the Corinthians. Some of the Romans have even been in the faith longer than Paul (16:7). He has long wanted to visit Rome but has not been able (1:9–13). Now he anticipates a trip to spread the gospel among the gentiles in Spain and hopes to stop in Rome on the way (15:22–29).

Although Paul lacks the firsthand knowledge that he has of his other audiences, his letter reveals a number of glimpses into the character of the community. Romans 16 is a veritable gold mine in this respect. Some are wealthy enough to own houses, while more than a dozen have names that are common among slaves. Seven of those named are women. Personal acquaintance with so many people in a city he has yet to visit suggests that many of Paul's readers are well traveled, and

---

3. For discussion of the issues surrounding authorship of Paul's letters, see chapter 6.

not only those to whom he refers as "co-workers." A few are "relatives" (*syngenēs*), which may reflect family ties or simply a shared Jewish heritage. High-profile readers include the first convert from the province of Asia (16:5) and Andronicus and Junia, "prominent among the apostles" (16:7; it is unclear whether this denotes their status as apostles or that they are well known to the other apostles).

Nonbiblical sources also contain valuable information about Roman Christianity and the circumstances facing the audience. Of special significance is the relationship between Jews and gentiles, a concern that runs through the letter from beginning (1:2–6) to end (16:26). At least a century before Paul, Roman writers attest to a large Jewish community in the capital (Cicero, *Pro Flacco* 28.66). The Jewish population when Paul is writing may be as high as fifty thousand.[4] As in other cities, Christianity in Rome almost certainly emerged first from within the Jewish community. Gentiles, including those already attracted to Judaism, begin to join the movement soon thereafter.

Roman authorities tended to be tolerant of foreign religions, but periodic outbreaks of anti-Semitic sentiment can be seen when they sensed a threat to the public peace. Multiple sources report that such a disturbance led Emperor Claudius to expel the Jews from Rome in 49 CE. (According to Acts 18:2, Prisca and Aquila were among the exiled Jews.) Suetonius (*Claudius* 25.4) says that the disturbance had something to do with a certain "Chrestus," a name that many scholars suspect is a garbled version of "Christus." If this is the case, it points to growing tensions between Jews who professed faith in Jesus and those who did not. Gentile influence within the church no doubt grew when the Jews departed. When Claudius died in 54, his edict was no longer enforced and Jews began to return.

This situation provides the likely context for Paul's letter. There are three different theories about the audience he envisions. One theory sees an exclusively Jewish Christian audience. Scholars who argue for this theory point to the emphasis on justification by faith and the inadequacy of Torah observance for gaining salvation, the abundant use of the Old Testament, and the reference to Abraham

4. H. J. Leon, *The Jews of Ancient Rome* (Philadelphia: Jewish Publication Society of America, 1960), 135–36.

as "our ancestor according to the flesh" (4:1). A second theory sees an exclusively gentile Christian audience. Supporters of this view also point to the emphasis on justification by faith but also to the specific references to the audience's role in a God-ordained mission to the gentiles (1:6, 13; 15:7–12, 15–16). Most persuasive is Paul's address "you Gentiles" at 11:13–32. A third theory sees a mixed, though predominantly gentile, audience. Paul directs many of his arguments to a Jewish interlocutor (e.g., 2:17–3:8; 9:1–5). This may simply be due to his use of the diatribe style, but the amount of space he devotes to Jewish objections seems too great if he is dealing with purely hypothetical challenges to his ministry.

The third possibility strikes most scholars as the likeliest. The bulk of the letter, and especially Rom. 9–11, aims at demonstrating how Jews and gentiles *together* comprise God's elect. To this lengthy theoretical discussion Paul adds more practical instructions designed to help these two factions coexist peacefully. He urges a group he calls "the strong" not to despise those he calls "the weak" (14:1–15:13). "The weak" are members who abstain from meat and wine and celebrate special holy days. "The strong" are those who regard such scrupulous observances as silly and superstitious. The weak are probably Jewish believers, while the strong are probably gentiles. Criticism of Jews in the ancient Mediterranean often focused on these very practices, and the mutual animosity that characterized Jew-gentile relations may not have been wiped away completely by the waters of baptism. Paul's counsel reflects heightened tensions within the group when Jewish believers returned to Rome after the death of Claudius.

Solidarity within the Christian community will be necessary if it is to survive even in the best of times. Paul's comments on submitting to the civil authorities serve as a reminder that the political climate could change with alarming speed (13:1–7). The fairness of Roman tax policies is a raging issue in the late 50s. Advising the Romans to pay "taxes to whom taxes are due," Paul thinks it wise to avoid attracting any unnecessary attention by appearing to shirk their civic duties. In a cruel twist of fate, the same emperor he tells the Romans to obey—Nero—will blame the Christians for the fire at Rome a few years later and have Paul executed.

99

1–2 Corinthians

No single source reveals more about life on the ground in early Christianity than the Corinthian correspondence. The wealth of information contained in these two letters makes it possible to form a fuller picture of this community than for any of Paul's other audiences, even if the details occasionally raise as many questions as they answer. First Corinthians presents a picture of a community divided along several fault lines. Paul spent eighteen months in Corinth after establishing the church there and then left for further mission work (Acts 18:1–11). In his absence, disputes arose on a number of matters. He writes 1 Corinthians to answer their questions.

With Chloe as his informant, he also gives guidance on matters about which they have remained conspicuously silent (1:11). Factions loyal to Apollos and Cephas have formed (1:12). Not everyone, it seems, regards Paul as their spiritual father, perhaps because Paul baptized only a few of them (1:14–16; 4:14–15). Most of the Corinthians are from the margins of society, a fact that makes the wisdom and spiritual gifts they have received all the more special to them (1:26–29; 3:18–19). Despite their new life in Christ, some old habits die hard. One couple is carrying on an incestuous relationship, and Paul is amazed that the church tolerates it (1 Cor. 5).[5] They are suing one another in the civil courts (6:1–8). Some men are still visiting prostitutes (6:15–20), not surprising, perhaps, given ancient Corinth's reputation for debauchery.

Answers to the questions contained in their earlier letter begin in 1 Cor. 7. Within the community, there are different opinions about the propriety of marriage and sexual activity, even within the bounds of marriage (1 Cor. 7). From Paul's discussion it is clear that the church in Corinth includes slave and free (7:21–24), Jew and gentile (7:17–20; 12:2), married (some to non-Christian spouses: 7:10–16) and unmarried (7:8–9, 25–28, 36–38), and widows as well (7:8, 39–40).

Eating of food sacrificed to idols is also causing problems (1 Cor. 8–10). Some see it as taboo because of its association with pagan

5. They appear to have misinterpreted an earlier comment of Paul's on a related subject (5:9–10). Depending on how one understands Paul's remark in 5:2, it may be that the Corinthians are even bragging about the couple as evidence of their liberation from bourgeois standards of morality.

worship. Others see no problem with it because, as believers in the one and only God, they put no stock in claims about supposed union with pagan deities. The dispute itself suggests that the group has not totally segregated itself from the larger culture, where the decision to eat or not to eat was unavoidable (cf. 10:25–30).

Dining practices of a different sort reveal other divisions in the church (11:17–34). It is their custom to gather at the home of a member and share a meal in memory of the Last Supper.[6] But the occasion has turned into a drinking party. Those able to arrive on time, moreover, go ahead and eat without waiting for their brothers and sisters who show up later, perhaps because their duties as household servants afford them less freedom. Rather than promoting unity within the body, then, these gatherings exacerbate tensions between members of different classes.

Corinthian worship practices and theological convictions also come into view. Women pray and prophesy in a manner that causes some consternation, possibly because their flowing locks too closely resemble the hairstyle of Greek priestesses (11:2–16). Speaking in tongues occurs on a regular basis (1 Cor. 14). When it is not done "decently and in order" (14:40), that is, without someone able to interpret the language that no one understands, Paul prefers that they focus on hymns, lessons, or revelations. Their observance of an otherwise unknown ritual is implied in an enigmatic reference to people "who receive baptism on behalf of the dead" (15:29). The lengthy discussion of the resurrection (15:1–57) hints at some confusion in Corinth about its centrality to Christian teaching.

Second Corinthians is addressed to the same congregation, though Paul adds "all the saints throughout Achaia" to the salutation (1:1). Contact with Paul has continued in the time since 1 Corinthians was delivered. They have received at least one more letter from Paul, a letter written "out of much distress and anguish of heart and with many tears" (2 Cor. 2:3–4). That letter followed a second, "painful visit" to Corinth that did not go very well (2:1). Rival teachers have planted seeds of doubt among the Corinthians concerning Paul's integrity and

6. Based on a study of Corinthian villas, Jerome Murphy-O'Connor estimates that the maximum occupancy of the houses where such gatherings took place would be around fifty; *St. Paul's Corinth: Texts and Archaeology*, 3rd ed. (Collegeville, MN: Liturgical Press, 2002), 182. Their meetings took place on Sundays (1 Cor. 16:2).

A Letter to Paul from Corinth?

What became of the letters sent to Paul by the Corinthian church? Much to the chagrin of historians, they have not survived. Included in the second-century *Acts of Paul*, however, is the text of a letter sent by the Corinthians to ask Paul's opinion about the "pernicious words" of two teachers, Simon and Cleobius.[1] Among their subversive teachings are claims that God is not almighty, that there is no resurrection of the body, that Christ never came in the flesh, and that the creation of the world was the work of angels instead of God. Paul refutes these doctrines in his response, which is also found in the *Acts of Paul*. Paul's response also circulated separately under the title *3 Corinthians*. Scholars believe the letters are not authentic but were fabricated to combat heretical ideas derived from 1–2 Corinthians by gnostics in the second century. The Corinthian letter and *3 Corinthians* were included in the New Testament canon of the Armenian church for several centuries.

1. For an English translation of this letter, see J. K. Elliott, *The Apocryphal New Testament* (Oxford: Oxford University Press, 2005), 380.

---

his worthiness as a minister of the gospel (2 Cor. 10–12). The audience may have witnessed a showdown between Paul and these so-called super-apostles (*hyperlian apostoloi*) that left them unimpressed with their founder (10:8–11; 11:5–6). This would account for Paul's defensive tone (e.g., 6:12; 11:7–9; 12:11–13, 19). Paul may also fear that the Corinthians are having second thoughts about the financial contribution they have promised to make to his mission (2 Cor. 8–9). He hopes this collection will serve as a symbol of unity between the predominantly gentile church at Corinth and the needy in the church at Jerusalem.

Galatians

A circular letter to "the churches of Galatia" (1:2) was probably meant to be read to multiple congregations by Paul's messenger. Because the name was used as an ethnic and as a political label, scholars disagree about the area in Asia Minor Paul has in mind. Is it northern Galatia, inhabited by a people of central European origin, or is it southern Galatia, a region also included within the official boundaries of the Roman province of Galatia? According to Acts, Paul and Barnabas planted churches in the south (13:14–14:26). Fortunately, it is unnecessary to locate the Galatians on a map in order to understand the letter Paul sends them.

While Paul never claims to be their founder, he undeniably speaks to the Galatians with an air of authority. He becomes very protective when he senses a danger to their faith. Paul and the Galatians have formed a strong bond. They showed him great hospitality and perhaps contributed to his collection for the poor at Jerusalem (4:14–15; cf. 1 Cor. 16:1). Disagreements between casual acquaintances do not erupt into the exasperation, sarcasm, and denunciations of the sort one finds here (e.g., 1:6–9; 4:15–20). Only close relationships evoke such harshness and expressions of betrayal.

What has come between Paul and the "foolish Galatians" (3:1)? Paul's impassioned defense of himself suggests that the Galatians have begun doubting his credentials as an apostle and the reliability of his teaching. Other teachers have arrived and proclaimed a message at odds with Paul's (1:6–8; 5:7). For Paul to combat false teaching is nothing out of the ordinary. The vehemence of his response, however, shows that this "different gospel" has gained traction among his readers.

"Formerly," Paul writes, they "did not know God" and "were enslaved to beings that by nature are not gods" (4:8). This description applies to gentiles, not Jewish Christians. The other teachers have, in Paul's absence, "bewitched" the Galatians (3:1), persuading them of the need to follow Jewish customs as a condition for salvation (4:21). Observing special rites and holy days (4:10), Paul fears that they are submitting to a "yoke of slavery" (5:1). After nearly two thousand years, the idea that a person would need to observe Jewish law in order to be a Christian may sound strange. But the gentiles of Galatia appear to have drawn that conclusion, prodded by Jewish Christian missionaries who argued that worship of the Jewish God made manifest in a Jewish messiah as prophesied in the Jewish scriptures might require the observation of Jewish law.

Chief among the customs the Galatians are being urged to adopt is circumcision (5:2–12; 6:12–15). Many gentiles in the ancient world were attracted to Judaism, but the requirement of circumcision quite understandably caused them to hesitate. Whatever their other faults, that the Galatians are seriously entertaining the idea of undergoing circumcision shows that fear of commitment is not among them.

Ephesians

Ephesians resembles Romans in the grand sweep of its theological vision. The two letters are also similar in that the author and audience have not met personally, though they are acquainted through other sources (Eph. 1:15; 3:2). Ephesians lacks the personal greetings found in the other Pauline letters. One also looks in vain for any details of local affairs in Ephesus. These facts are surprising in light of Acts 20, which depicts the relationship between Paul and the Ephesian Christians as a tender one that developed over a three-year period. More telling still, the words "in Ephesus" (Eph. 1:1) are missing from the earliest and most reliable manuscripts of the letter. For these reasons, it appears that the intended audience of Ephesians does not consist, at least not exclusively, of flesh-and-blood Ephesians. It is not implausible to think of Ephesians as a sort of circular letter, like 1 Peter, sent to multiple churches in Asia Minor.

The author addresses the readers as "Gentiles" (2:11–12; 3:1; cf. 4:17). There is no sign of the Jew-gentile friction so prevalent in Acts and Romans. The "dividing wall" of hostility appears to be a thing of the past (2:13–20). The emphasis on the role of the uncircumcised in God's eternal plan (1:4–11; 3:5–6) would resonate with gentiles troubled by the idea that their inclusion in the people of God might have been an afterthought. The "household code" in 5:22–6:8 implies the presence of wives, husbands, children, slaves, and masters. Allusions throughout the letter to baptism (1:13; 4:5, 30; 5:8, 26) may function as reminders for recent converts still discovering the full meaning of their commitment to lead a new life.

A majority of scholars believe that Paul is not the author of Ephesians. Because the letter speaks to a very general rather than to a particular audience, certainty about the identity of the author would furnish little additional information about the original readers.

Philippians

"All the saints . . . in Philippi" (1:1) reside in a major city in the region of Macedonia. Thanks to Shakespeare, Philippi is remembered today as the site of the battle at which Mark Antony and Octavian (later Augustus) defeated the conspirators responsible for the murder of Julius Caesar. To honor the colony, Augustus Caesar granted the residents Roman citizenship, which came with privileges not accorded to other cities in the empire, such as exemption from tribute and taxes. This special status likely informs Paul's argument when he reminds them that their "citizenship" (*politeuma*) is in heaven and not in any earthly city (3:20). They are to "conduct themselves" (*politeuesthe*) accordingly, he says in 1:27, using politically charged language that is difficult to capture in English translation.

Mentioned in the salutation are "bishops" (*episkopoi*) and "deacons" (*diakonoi*). Whether one prefers these terms or the less formal "overseers" and "helpers," it appears that the Philippians have developed at least a rudimentary hierarchy within the community. Little can be said about this organization except that women play a role in it. Euodia and Syntyche appear as two of Paul's coworkers (4:2–3). These women are at odds over some unspecified matter. That Paul sees fit to single them out and plead for their reconciliation suggests that their disagreement is not a purely private affair but one that affects the whole group. The prominence of women in the community agrees with the account of the church's founding in Acts 16, where Lydia and her household become Paul's first converts in Philippi.

The Philippians have exhibited extraordinary generosity. To acknowledge the gifts they have sent via Epaphroditus is one of Paul's reasons for writing (Phil. 4:18). From the earliest days of the ministry in Europe they have opened their hearts and wallets to Paul. They were the only church to share with Paul "in the matter of giving and receiving," sending aid repeatedly even when he was in Thessalonica (4:15–16). Paul goes so far as to hold them up as an example to the Corinthians (2 Cor. 8:1–6). They "voluntarily gave according to their means, and even beyond their means, begging us earnestly for the privilege of sharing in this ministry to the saints." The tone of joy and gratitude that pervades Philippians is no doubt a result of this enthusiastic response on the part of the audience.

The note in 2 Corinthians about a "severe ordeal" confirms the suspicion that the Philippians are facing some sort of persecution (Phil. 1:27–30). Paul's reflections on his own imprisonment (1:12–26) generate solidarity with his audience in their sufferings. (It may also be that Paul wants to help them through the potential embarrassment of having a spiritual leader who is constantly being incarcerated.) The precise nature of the harassment is not clear. Warnings about "those who mutilate the flesh" (3:2) and Paul's emphasis on his own Jewish bona fides may indicate a Jewish opposition. There is little archaeological evidence for a sizable Jewish presence in Philippi. The official imperial cult, on the other hand, was firmly established, as was the worship of various deities such as Isis, Serapis, Cybele, Juno, Minerva, Mars, and Diana. These factors, along with the scarcity of Old Testament citations, lead many scholars to conclude that the Philippians as well as their opponents are predominantly gentile.

Stress connected to persecution from outside often takes its toll on internal relations. Paul's repeated admonitions that they "have the same mind" imply that Euodia and Syntyche are not the only sources of strife (2:1–4, 14; 4:2–3).

Colossians

Colossae was located in the Lycus River valley in western Asia Minor. There is no record of Paul having visited the city. Epaphras, not Paul, was probably the founder of the Colossian church (1:7; 4:12; cf. 2:1). The restrained rhetoric of the letter may be due to this lack of a personal relationship. Paul's authorship is disputed by many scholars. In this instance, however, the profile of the audience changes very little on the basis of the author's identity. Whether Paul writes it in the 50s or someone else does later in the first century, the audience knows Paul only indirectly but holds him in sufficiently high regard to find the letter worth reading and preserving for posterity.

The Colossians have been "rescued . . . from the power of darkness" (1:13). They "were once estranged and hostile in mind" (1:21) and formerly "were dead in trespasses and the uncircumcision of [their] flesh" (2:13). These remarks point to a gentile background. Instructions directed to wives, husbands, children, slaves, and masters give evidence of social diversity within the group (3:18–4:1; slaves receive the most extensive instructions). Paul warns the Colossians about those who would deceive them "through philosophy and empty deceit" (2:4, 8). This vaguely described threat may have its source in pagan mystery religions or Jewish mysticism. The relative lack of urgency in Paul's warnings is perhaps a sign that it has yet to make significant headway in the community.

Colossians 4 contains a number of personal greetings that reveal a glimpse into the community's social network. Paul assumes regular contact between the churches at Colossae and Laodicea, located about ten miles down the road (4:15–16). The Colossians are acquainted with several named individuals out in the mission field with the apostle. In this group is Onesimus, who Paul says is "one of them" (4:9). In addition to Onesimus, most of the names appearing in Philemon also appear here. The audiences of these two letters are thus familiar with one another. (If Colossians is a pseudonymous composition, the overlap between the two strongly implies that the letter to Philemon is well known to the intended audience of Colossians.)

1–2 Thessalonians

If the scholarly consensus about the date of 1 Thessalonians is correct, the Christians in Macedonia's largest city may be Paul's earliest readers. Acts 17 and 1 Thess. 2:2 agree in depicting Paul as the

---

The Laodicean Letter

Paul tells the Colossians to make sure they read a letter he has sent to the Laodiceans (Col. 4:16). As early as the second century, writers puzzled over this reference. Marcion thought that the canonical book of Ephesians was the actual letter to which Paul refers. A few modern scholars theorize that Hebrews or Philemon may be the letter Paul has in mind. Most scholars now believe that any letter from Paul to Laodicea has been lost.

At least one ancient writer, however, was not so easily discouraged and decided to take matters into his own hands. A brief epistle "To the Laodiceans" was in circulation during the fourth century and perhaps earlier.[1] Its anonymous author strung together several generic Pauline phrases, drawn largely from Galatians and Philippians, and in the last line urged the Laodiceans to read the letter to the Colossians. The temptation to continue the conversation proved hard to resist when a convenient opportunity presented itself, even if the unknown author had nothing terribly interesting to add to the mix.

1. For an English translation of this letter, see Bart D. Ehrman, *Lost Scriptures: Books That Did Not Make It into the New Testament* (Oxford: Oxford University Press, 2003), 165–66.

---

founder of this church. Their number may include Jews, but the majority comes from a gentile background. When they converted to Christianity, they "turned to God from idols, to serve a living and true God" (1:9). They have also endured ill treatment from their pagan neighbors (2:14), perhaps for their perceived aloofness in a city invested in the Roman imperial cult and alive with the worship of Greek and Egyptian deities. Membership includes manual laborers, among whom Paul toiled when he was in the city (2:9; 4:11). His comment to the Philippians that they provided much-needed financial assistance while he was in Thessalonica (Phil. 4:16) is independent evidence of their position toward the lower end of the socioeconomic ladder.

Paul wants the letter to be read to the entire community (1 Thess. 5:27). That Paul bothers to state this command makes one pause. He appears to anticipate a smaller circle reading the letter—perhaps the leadership that has already emerged (5:12–13)—before it is shared with the group as a whole.[7] His tone is affectionate because he wants to provide encouragement to a church that is still very young in the faith.

Faith, hope, and love are the three criteria by which Paul assesses the audience. From Timothy he has learned that they excel in the areas of faith and love (1:8; 3:6–7; 4:9–10). Hope is where they fall short. Although they have received instruction about the end times (5:1–2), they have begun to despair for some of their fellow believers who have died before Jesus's second coming (4:13–18). Will these dearly departed brethren miss out on the full realization of the kingdom? It is to correct any misunderstandings on this point that Paul writes 1 Thessalonians.

Evidence from the text of 2 Thessalonians adds to this picture, though many scholars wonder whether Paul is its true author. If Paul is the author, the Thessalonians receive this second letter soon after the first. Persecution already under way when 1 Thessalonians was written has gone from bad to worse (2 Thess. 1:4–10). This heightened persecution has made their worries about the end times even more acute (2:1–2). But their grasp of such esoteric matters is faulty (2:3–12). Paul is perplexed that they have forgotten or misunderstood what he

7. Cf. Abraham J. Malherbe, *The Letters to the Thessalonians*, Anchor Bible 32B (New York: Doubleday, 2000), 353–55.

has previously taught them (2:5, 15). In retrospect, it is understandable that his explanation in 1 Thess. 4:13–5:11—the coming of the Lord will be "like a thief in the night"!—did not succeed in putting their minds at ease.

Some of the Thessalonians have also taken his call to watchfulness too literally. They are devoting themselves to reading the signs of the times instead of doing good works or, indeed, doing any work at all (2 Thess. 3:6–13). What point is there in working, after all, when the world may end before payday? To the idle, his command is the same as it was before he left for Athens: "Anyone unwilling to work should not eat" (3:10).

If Paul is not the author of 2 Thessalonians, some aspects of this portrait change but others do not. If a different person writes it but with Paul's approval and during Paul's lifetime, then nothing really changes. The intended audience in either scenario is familiar with 1 Thessalonians and regards Paul as an authoritative teacher. They are anxious due to the perceived delay of the second coming. On the hypothesis that 2 Thessalonians is a pseudonymous composition written late in the first century, it is unlikely that the actual readers the author has in view are located in Thessalonica (or else they would be suspicious about a letter meant for them that turns up after getting "lost in the mail" for about forty years).

The Pastoral Epistles (1–2 Timothy and Titus)

Questions about authorship, genre, and audience are more closely linked for the Pastoral Epistles than for Paul's other letters. Most scholars view 1–2 Timothy and Titus as pseudonymous documents written decades after Paul's death. Timothy and Titus, accordingly, are not seen as the actual readers. Those who reject Pauline authorship typically regard the Pastoral Epistles as a single production divided into three parts. Those who accept Pauline authorship see them as three separate letters addressing three distinct situations sent to two of Paul's closest associates.

If Timothy and Titus are not the intended recipients, the author has a more general audience in mind rather than some other individual(s) who remain nameless. Addressing these "letters" to well-known figures is a literary conceit. It allows the wider audience to whom the author is really speaking to overhear "Paul" communicating with his most trusted coworkers. On the surface, the author appears to be giving personal advice to pastors dealing with thorny problems that have arisen in their congregations. But if the author is writing privately to particular church leaders of a later generation, there would be little point in pretending to be Paul. The purpose of the Pauline pseudonym as well as the fabricated details about Timothy and Titus, therefore, is to lend weight to the letters' instructions in the eyes of communities who respect Paul and would trust his opinions on hotly contested questions.[8]

In the prevailing approach to the Pastoral Epistles, these controversies help to identify the true audience. Exposure to false teaching worries the author (1 Tim. 1:3–8; 6:3–5, 20; 2 Tim. 2:14–18; Titus 1:10–16; 3:9–11). Specific details about false teachers are few, but many scholars see similarities to gnostic ideas about the material world. The author says these "liars" forbid marriage and demand abstinence from certain foods and in response affirms the goodness of God's creation (1 Tim. 4:1–5).

There are also indications that the author is concerned about the authority and behavior of women in the church (1 Tim. 2:8–15). From the command to keep silent and to remain in submission to male authority, it is plausible to assume that some women are teaching in the church and perhaps aspiring to positions of leadership. Behind the extended discussion of widows (5:3–16) some see evidence for an order of female itinerant preachers like Thecla, who appears in the second-century *Acts of Paul and Thecla*. It is not clear which group constitutes the author's primary target audience, those who champion a radical Paul or the orthodox seeking to keep radical movements in check.

To maintain order in the face of potentially crippling divisions, the author seeks to validate the hierarchy of bishops and deacons (1 Tim.

8. It is widely thought that the audience's admiration for Paul comes from having read the Acts of the Apostles. Not so widely accepted is Jerome D. Quinn's theory that the Pastoral Epistles constitute Luke's "third volume," with the implication that the intended audience for the Gospel of Luke and Acts is the same as that for the Pastoral Epistles; see "The Last Volume of Luke: The Relation of Luke-Acts to the Pastoral Epistles," in *Perspectives on Luke-Acts*, ed. C. H. Talbert (Danville, VA: Association of Baptist Professors of Religion, 1978), 62–75.

3:1–13; Titus 1:5–9). First Timothy and Titus assume an administrative structure that is not as evident in Paul's other writings. This bureaucracy is what leads many scholars to date these letters to the second century, when conflicting understandings of Paul's teachings have appeared. The intended audience may be dubious about the legitimacy of the authority they exercise.

If Paul is the author of the Pastoral Epistles, identifying the audiences requires less guesswork. Timothy is Paul's most trusted colleague and collaborator (cf. Acts 18:5; 1 Cor. 4:17; Phil. 2:19–24; 1 Thess. 3:2). His mother Eunice is Jewish but his father is not (Acts 16:1–3; 2 Tim. 1:5). In person he is apparently underwhelming (1 Cor. 16:10–11; 1 Tim. 4:12; 2 Tim. 1:7), due perhaps to his youth or to a weak constitution (1 Tim. 4:12; 5:23). Little wonder he needs encouragement when he is dispatched to supervise a contentious group in a large, cosmopolitan city (1:3–4).

The Ephesian church to which Timothy has been sent has been in existence long enough to develop a system of leadership (3:1–13; depending on how one interprets 3:11, this system may include women). Among Timothy's assignments is to ensure that these leadership posts are filled by the most qualified candidates. Accusations of wrongdoing have been leveled against some leaders (5:19–20). There is also some dispute about appropriate compensation for elders and teachers (5:17–18). Management of the church's assistance to widows, both young and old, appears to present the biggest logistical problem (5:3–16). Taken all together, these matters bear witness to a diverse, thriving, sometimes unruly group of considerable yet finite resources coming to terms with the practical realities of life in community.

Titus is a gentile (Gal. 2:1–3). He has helped Paul in his dealings with the Corinthians (2 Cor. 7:6, 13–14; 8:6, 23). Paul has left him in charge of the church on the island of Crete, where, like Timothy, he is contending with opposing teachers (Titus 1:5, 10–11). It is a fledgling congregation; because the Cretans are so new to the faith, he cannot count on all potential elders to have families that are fully Christian (1:6). The church at Crete is multigenerational. Family relations within the households—if the specific instructions Titus is to deliver are any indication (2:1–10)—are less than ideal. How closely they conform to the stereotype of Cretans as "always liars, vicious brutes, lazy gluttons" (1:12) is hard to say.

It has been suggested that 1 Timothy and Titus belong to the literary genre *mandata principis*. This would explain the way in which these letters alternate between a public and a private audience. Letters in this genre are sent by a superior to a representative and contain instructions on the representative's mission. The audience of such letters includes the newly appointed delegate, who receives needed validation from the superior, and also the constituency to which he has been sent, who then have some means by which to assess the performance of the delegate. The author, be it Paul or someone else, is therefore addressing not only his faithful coworkers but also the sheep in the flocks they have been asked to tend.

Philemon

The shortest Pauline letter is not quite as private and personal as its title suggests. Along with Philemon, Paul addresses Apphia, Archippus, and the church that meets at Philemon's home (2). A runaway slave, Onesimus, is the subject of the letter.

Philemon is a wealthy man. He owns a house large enough to accommodate church meetings as well as overnight guests (22). He may be a financial contributor to Paul's ministry (4–7), in which case he acts as Paul's patron and benefactor. This might account for the deferential tone Paul adopts. But Philemon owes some debt to Paul too; when Paul says that Philemon owes him "even [his] own self" (19), he may be reminding Philemon that he is the one who converted him to Christianity. Their relationship, then, is anything but simple and straightforward.

Paul hopes that Philemon will remain his "partner" (17). What does this entail? Most scholars believe that Paul is asking Philemon to welcome back Onesimus, who has become a Christian, and free him from slavery or, at least, not punish him for escaping. It is unclear precisely what Paul expects of Philemon because he is so indirect. This indirectness has much to do with the delicate nature of the situation. As a slave owner in Roman society, Philemon has certain rights, and freeing a slave meant forfeiting a substantial investment (which, in turn, would affect Philemon's ability to act as a host to the church and a financial supporter of Paul). Hard as it is for modern readers to fathom, moreover, it was hardly self-evident to Christians that slavery was inherently evil. Virtually everyone in the ancient world saw it as an inevitable part of the natural order of things.

This is where the other audience members come into the picture. "Sister" Apphia may be Philemon's biological sister, a sister "in Christ," or perhaps his wife. Little else is known about Archippus or "the church in [Philemon's] house." Their inclusion in the greeting is not simply a polite gesture. The use of the plural pronoun "you" in 22 and 25 ("you guys" or "y'all" in English) indicates that Paul expects them to be privy to the letter's contents. By speaking to a broader audience, Paul is inviting others to hold Philemon accountable for the decision he makes in response to Paul's request. Any other slaves in Philemon's household, Christian or pagan, would also be extremely curious about Philemon's decision.

How did Philemon respond? The only clue is found in someone seeing fit to preserve the letter and copy it for other readers. Does this hint at a happy resolution to an awkward dilemma?

Conclusion

It goes without saying that disclosing information about his readers to third parties is not among Paul's chief concerns. For this very reason, however, the incidental details gleaned from a close reading of the letters are all the more revealing. Diligent readers can gather heaps of data that shed much-needed light on matters concealed from plain view due to the passage of time.

But even the cleverest of readers face certain challenges in trying to construct a general profile of Paul's readers.

First, grasping the message of a letter depends on knowing something about the audience, but how one envisions an audience is in part a function of what one thinks the author is trying to say and do. Only with great care is it possible to avoid circular reasoning.

Second, it is possible that Paul's familiarity with his own readers is less than complete. He states that he has yet to visit the church at

Rome (Rom. 15:22–24), which means that he cannot know them as well as he knows the Corinthians or the Philippians. Suspicious of his biases, some scholars go further and mistrust what Paul implies about his audiences. If Paul actually hoped to convince his readers to see things as he saw them, however, he could hardly afford to distort the facts too egregiously when writing them.

Third, reading between the lines to discover facts about the world behind the text of letters written long ago will rarely, if ever, bring absolute certainty about the context of the readers. A more recent example illustrates how easy it is to err in this respect. In the 1998 movie *Saving Private Ryan*, General George Marshall learns that the title character, who has stormed the beaches at Normandy on D-Day, has three brothers who have already died in combat. He reads to his assembled staff a letter written in 1864 by Abraham Lincoln concerning a similar situation and issues an order to find the surviving brother and bring him home. The scene is fictional but the letter is not. Lincoln's moving letter to Mrs. Lydia Bixby is often referred to as the most famous letter in American history:

> I have been shown in the files of the War Department a statement of the Adjutant General of Massachusetts that you are the mother of five sons who have died gloriously on the field of battle. I feel how weak and fruitless must be any word of mine which should attempt to beguile you from the grief of a loss so overwhelming. But I cannot refrain from tendering you the consolation that may be found in the thanks of the Republic they died to save. I pray that our Heavenly Father may assuage the anguish of your bereavement, and leave you only the cherished memory of the loved and lost, and the solemn pride that must be yours to have laid so costly a sacrifice upon the altar of freedom.

From this brief note one might reasonably conclude that the bereaving Mrs. Bixby has five sons, that they fought zealously for the Union cause, and that they died in battle. Historians have cast doubt on these conclusions. Bixby did have five sons, but it appears that three of them survived the war. Of the survivors, one deserted the Union army, one was captured by the Confederacy, and one was honorably discharged. Contemporary sources suggest she may have lied about her sons in order to receive financial assistance from the government. It is also thought that Bixby, who had moved to Boston from Richmond, was a Confederate sympathizer. Her great-grandson claims that she tore up the letter in anger after reading it.[9]

For these reasons, interpretations of the letters based upon assumptions about their original audiences should remain provisional in the absence of supporting evidence. Asking questions about the audience nevertheless serves as a valuable device for readers who want to absorb more from the letters and their context than they might from an otherwise casual reading. Making an effort to reconstruct those audiences in their contexts prevents modern readers from projecting alien questions and concerns onto the texts.

Although this volume promotes literary and historical strategies for reading Paul's letters, it is instructive to recall that the overwhelming majority of Paul's readers for the last nineteen centuries have been readers about whom Paul knew nothing. It would be a mistake, however, to imagine that this eavesdropping is a peculiarly modern breach of decorum. From a very early date, people other than Paul's intended audiences have been reading the letters. Most of the letters were originally sent to specific groups or individuals, but all of the earliest manuscripts that survive include not individual letters but, rather, collections of letters. In other words, as far back as we have physical evidence, whoever was reading the Letter to the Galatians was probably reading most of the other letters as well. Clement of Rome and Ignatius of Antioch, writing their own letters at the end of the first and beginning of the second century, quote frequently from several of Paul's writings, which means that they have read copies of them. The author of 2 Peter mentions "all [Paul's] letters" and indicates that he is not alone in having read them (3:15–16). The development of Christianity as a cohesive religious movement not limited to a particular time or place is partly a result of this practice of reading other people's mail. Believers in Antioch and Ephesus and Corinth saw that they shared the same hopes and fears, and so they treated Paul's letters as possessing a relevance that transcended the circumstances that first prompted their composition. A sense of a

9. Michael Burlingame, "New Light on the Bixby Letter," *Journal of the Abraham Lincoln Association* 16.1 (1995): 59–72.

common identity emerged and grew as they copied and exchanged the letters they had received, as if forwarding emails they found especially witty or wise.

How early did this process begin? Did Paul himself aim at or anticipate a readership wider than the headings of his letters would seem to suggest? Other New Testament epistles such as James and 1 Peter show that he would not have been alone in doing so. *When* Paul's letters began to circulate among Christian communities and *by whose initiative* are questions with no certain answers.[10] Either the author or the audience(s) authorized the wider dissemination of the letters. The author of Colossians wants the letter to be read at Laodicea and also wants the Colossians to read "the letter from Laodicea" (4:16). If Paul is the author of Colossians, then this practice begins very early indeed.[11]

Did Paul deliberately write for a general audience in some cases but not others? Do any elements of the letter(s) reflect this purpose? Did he arrange for them to be distributed more widely only at a later date, in which case the original composition is best read as a piece of private correspondence? There is perhaps no uniform solution to the historical riddles the Pauline letters present. Answers to these questions vary according to the letter. Keeping the questions in view will facilitate more incisive readings of the letters even if comprehensive answers ultimately remain out of reach.

·························· **For Further Discussion** ··························

1. What information about his intended audiences do Paul's letters furnish? What sorts of information cannot be had simply from reading the letters?

10. For a review of the various theories, see Harry Y. Gamble, *The New Testament Canon: Its Making and Meaning*, Guides to Biblical Scholarship (Philadelphia: Fortress, 1985), 35–41. See also Lucetta Mowrey, "The Early Circulation of Paul's Letters," *Journal of Biblical Literature* 63 (1944): 73–86.

11. David Trobisch argues that, even if Colossians is pseudonymous, Paul himself collected and edited Romans, 1–2 Corinthians, and Galatians for a broader audience; see *Paul's Letter Collection: Tracing the Origins* (Minneapolis: Fortress, 1994), 55–96.

2. In the case of the disputed letters that many scholars believe were written by someone other than Paul, how does one go about determining the identity of the intended audience?

3. To what degree and in what ways is it necessary to know about the audience to understand Paul's letters? Does the answer vary according to the letter in question?

For Further Reading

Adams, Edward, and David G. Horrell, eds. *Christianity at Corinth: The Quest for the Pauline Church*. Louisville: Westminster John Knox, 2004.

Barclay, John M. G. "Paul, Philemon, and the Dilemma of Christian Slave-Ownership." *New Testament Studies* 37 (1991): 161–86.

Barton, S. "Paul and Philemon: A Correspondence Continued." *Theology* 90 (1987): 97–101.

Bassler, Jouette. "The Widow's Tale: A Fresh Look at 1 Timothy 5:3–16." *Journal of Biblical Literature* 103 (1984): 23–41.

Dahl, Nils A. "The Particularity of the Pauline Epistles as a Problem in the Ancient Church." In *Neotestamentica et Patristica: Eine Freundesgabe, Herrn Professor Dr. Oscar Cullmann zu seinem 60. Geburtstag überreicht*, edited by W. C. van Unnik, 261–71. Novum Testamentum Supplement 6. Leiden: Brill, 1962.

Das, A. Andrew. *Solving the Romans Debate*. Minneapolis: Fortress, 2007.

Donfried, Karl P., ed. *The Romans Debate*. Rev. ed. Peabody, MA: Hendrickson, 1991.

Francis, Fred O., and Wayne A. Meeks, eds. *Conflict at Colossae*. Society of Biblical Literature Sources for Biblical Study 4. Missoula, MT: Society of Biblical Literature, 1973.

Johnson, Luke T. *Letters to Paul's Delegates: A Commentary on 1 Timothy, 2 Timothy, and Titus*. New Testament in Context. Valley Forge, PA: Trinity, 1996.

Koester, Helmut, ed. *Ephesos, Metropolis of Asia: An Interdisciplinary Approach to Its Archaeology, Religion, and Culture*. Harvard Theological Series 41. Valley Forge, PA: Trinity, 1995.

Malherbe, Abraham J. *Paul and the Thessalonians*. Philadelphia: Fortress, 1983.

Meeks, Wayne A. *The First Urban Christians: The Social World of the Apostle Paul*. New Haven: Yale University Press, 1983.

Mitchell, Margaret M. "New Testament Envoys in the Context of Greco-Roman Diplomatic and Epistolary Conventions: The Example of Timothy and Titus." *Journal of Biblical Literature* 111 (1992): 641–62.

Nanos, Mark D. *The Galatians Debate: Contemporary Issues in Rhetorical and Historical Interpretation.* Peabody, MA: Hendrickson, 2002.

Smith, Abraham. *Comfort One Another: Reconstructing the Rhetoric and Audience of 1 Thessalonians.* Louisville: Westminster John Knox, 1995.

Theissen, G. *The Social Setting of Pauline Christianity: Essays on Corinth.* Philadelphia: Fortress, 1982.

Thomas, W. D. "The Place of Women in the Church at Philippi." *Expository Times* 83 (1972): 117–20.

5

How Paul Reads the Old Testament

Casual readers may be forgiven for thinking of the Bible as one very long book. Its separate books appear together in a single volume, printed in the same font on the same tissue-thin paper, and written in the same biblical style. Literary style in one language is difficult to replicate in another, and thus the perception of a homogeneous style in the Bible is somewhat misleading. It is partly a result of a process in which a single translator or committee of translators renders the various texts into the target language. But only partly. The stylistic similarities between the Old Testament and the New Testament owe in no small part to the latter quoting the former so frequently. The earliest Christian writers quote or allude to the Jewish scriptures hundreds of times. It is impossible to make sense of their writings apart from their engagement with the Old Testament.

Paul is no exception to this rule. His language is the language of Scripture. Millions of Christians have for centuries regarded Paul's letters as holy writ, but Paul did not look at his letters in this way. When he sits down to write, he does not think, "What the Bible needs is another book or two!" "All scripture is inspired by God," he (or one of his followers) writes in 2 Tim. 3:16, "and is useful for teaching, for reproof, for correction, and for training in righteousness." Although he surely feels that they are useful for teaching, reproof, correction, and training in righteousness, his own letters do not belong to the category of Scripture until much later.[1] In the middle of the first century, that title applies exclusively to the Law, the Prophets, and the Writings, of which Paul was a dedicated reader.

The notion that the Word of God and the words of Scripture are one and the same is explicit in many Pauline texts (Rom. 9:17; Gal. 3:8). Paul regards Scripture as inspired. So, too, do his readers, or else he would have little reason to expect that they would find his Scripture-based claims compelling. "Inspiration" is an oft-used but typically ill-defined term. Does Paul's manner of referring to the Old Testament suggest that he regards it as prophetic? Yes and no. Paul shares with other New Testament writers the belief that Christians are living in a special era, somewhere between the inauguration of God's kingdom and its ultimate consummation. It is Paul's audacious claim that the church is the agent by which "the plan of the mystery hidden for ages in God" (Eph. 3:9) has finally been made known. Not only is the church uniquely qualified to explicate the Scriptures, but it is also the subject of the Scriptures. Unknown to themselves, it would seem, the prophets of old were actually speaking of the events surrounding the life, death, and resurrection of Jesus and the declaration of the good news to the nations (cf. Rom. 1:2; Heb. 1:1–2; 1 Pet. 1:10–12).

How did Paul arrive at this understanding of the Old Testament and its relation to the early church? And how does it come to expression in his letters? It does not happen as one sees in the closing scenes of the 1965 movie *The Greatest Story Ever Told*. On Easter morning, Mary Magdalene literally wakes up, suddenly remembers Jesus's predictions of his death and resurrection, and then rushes to the tomb to see if they have come true. The early Christian experience of Jesus being no longer among the dead by all accounts

---

1. How much later is a matter of debate. The author of 2 Peter says that "the ignorant and unstable twist" the meaning of Paul's letters "as they do the other scriptures" (3:16). The date of 2 Peter and the precise meaning of *graphē* are unclear. If *graphē* refers to "the scriptures" and not just other "writings," then Paul's letters may have been accorded canonical status by the end of the first century.

came as a shock and a surprise. The New Testament suggests that Hollywood gets this backward. Even if the historical Jesus prophesied such events, his disciples did not seem to understand (Mark 8:31–33; John 2:22).

Paul does not read the Old Testament and then try to make sense of Jesus. To the contrary, he has an experience of Jesus as the risen Lord and then rereads the Old Testament in the light of this experience. In the Gospel of Luke, the risen Jesus interprets for two disciples "the things about himself in all the scriptures" (24:27). They had been on the lookout for the Messiah, and even they fail to recognize him—literally and figuratively—until he explains "all that the prophets have declared" (24:17–25). Like these disciples, Paul rereads the Old Testament and sees, because of Jesus, things that he had not seen before and that Jews had not previously considered messianic prophecies. The impetus to search the Scriptures comes from the questions about the difference Jesus makes that arise in Paul's correspondence with his churches.

The Old Testament in Paul's Letters

Although Paul's technique is not uniform or systematic, asking a standard set of questions sheds light on his use of the Old Testament. The following sections discuss the issues these questions raise:

1. To what Old Testament text(s) does Paul refer in a given passage?
2. Does the wording of Paul's citation correspond exactly to the Old Testament passage? Does he modify the quotation in any way? Are there any evident reasons for the modification?
3. What is the original context of the passage in its Old Testament setting? Does Paul's use of this passage reflect an awareness of the original setting?
4. How does the Old Testament passage function in Paul's argument? Why is Paul using this particular Old Testament text?[2]

2. Adapted from Richard B. Hays and Joel B. Green, "The Use of the Old Testament by New Testament Writers," in *Hearing the New Testament: Strategies for Interpretation*, ed. Joel B. Green (Grand Rapids: Eerdmans, 1995), 232.

Quotations, Allusions, and Echoes

Before assessing Paul's use of the Old Testament, it is necessary to determine when and where he is referring to a specific text. References take various forms. Paul can quote a specific, identifiable text more or less verbatim. He can allude to a text without reproducing its precise language in any substantial or sustained fashion. And he can echo a theme or concept found in one or more Old Testament passages without giving any clear indication that he has a specific text in mind.

Paul quotes the Old Testament approximately one hundred times. Estimates vary, if only slightly, because it is not always clear when he is quoting a specific text. Paul frequently uses an introductory formula, "as it is written," to signal a biblical quotation (e.g., Rom. 1:17; 2:24; 2 Cor. 8:15; 9:9); occasionally he names the book from which a line is taken (e.g., Rom. 9:25); but typically there is nothing more than verbatim or near-verbatim correspondence to a known Old Testament text to tell the reader that Paul is quoting a biblical source. He sometimes combines lines from different texts into a longer string of quotations without using quotation marks to distinguish between the different sources (3:10–18). To complicate matters further, there are a few quotations for which Paul uses an introductory formula but the quoted text is not to be found in the Old Testament (1 Cor. 2:9; Eph. 4:8; 5:14). If only he had used some ancient version of *The Chicago Manual of Style*, identifying Paul's sources would not present so many problems!

Several quotations appear in Romans, 1–2 Corinthians, and Galatians; Ephesians contains just a few quotations; 1–2 Timothy contain one each; and Philippians, Colossians, 1–2 Thessalonians, and Titus contain none. His favorite texts to cite are, in order of frequency, Isaiah, Psalms, Genesis, and Deuteronomy, but he also quotes from the rest of the Pentateuch, 2 Samuel, 1 Kings, Job, Proverbs, Jeremiah, Ezekiel, Hosea, Joel, Habakkuk, and Malachi. This distribution is comparable to what one sees elsewhere in the New Testament. A number of key texts in Paul's arguments are quoted also by other New Testament authors (e.g., Gen. 2:24 in 1 Cor. 6:16 and Mark 10:7–8; Gen. 15:6 in Rom. 4:3 and James 2:23; Deut. 19:15 in 2 Cor. 13:1 and Matt. 18:16; Isa. 53:1 in Rom. 10:16 and John 12:38).

Allusions and echoes abound. It is not possible to give a precise number of Old Testament allusions in the Pauline letters because, in many cases, the allusion is not a discrete, self-contained reference. For example, in 2 Cor. 3:7–18 nearly every verse alludes to the story of Moses's return from Sinai with the two tablets of the law in Exod. 34:29–35. Should this count as a single allusion or several? However one enumerates them, the figure for all the letters reaches well into the hundreds. Among the texts to which Paul makes regular reference are the creation stories in Gen. 2, the Abraham cycle in Gen. 12–22, descriptions of Moses and the law in Exodus and Deuteronomy, and passages in the prophets that mention gentiles. That Paul alludes to the Old Testament so often should come as no surprise insofar as Paul is writing as a Jew to encourage his readers as they live out their faith in a Jewish messiah. That he does so even in letters to groups comprised predominantly of gentiles is a reminder that he is writing letters and not historical surveys or doctrinal overviews for a general audience. Gentiles among Paul's readers would have been catechized in the faith to some degree. If the letters were written as missionary sermons intended for gentiles uninstructed and uninitiated in the faith, extensive quotation of biblical texts would likely prove ineffective in achieving Paul's goal.

The line between echo and allusion can be a fine one. An echo is less distinct, less clear in its reference to a text. The author himself may not even be conscious of the influence of a certain text on his thought or expression. It is obvious, for example, that in Gal. 4:21–31 Paul is thinking of the stories about Sarah and Hagar in Genesis, even though he quotes only a line or two. Notwithstanding the arguments of Tertullian and many modern scholars, it is less obvious that Paul is thinking of the improper mating of "the sons of God" with "the daughters of humans" in Gen. 6:4 when he instructs female prophets to cover their heads "because of the angels" in 1 Cor. 11:10.

Arbitrary decisions about the presence of an allusion or echo can lead to misunderstandings of Paul's message in his letters. Richard B. Hays proposes seven criteria by which to distinguish an authentic allusion or echo from a false "discovery":

1. Availability: is it chronologically possible for Paul to have known the source?
2. Volume: are the similarities in language both numerous and distinctive?

3. Recurrence: does Paul quote or allude to the text elsewhere?

4. Thematic coherence: how well does the alleged allusion fit with Paul's line of thought?

5. Historical plausibility: is it conceivable that Paul could have intended the meaning implied by the apparent allusion, or would such a reading be anachronistic?

6. History of interpretation: have other readers over the centuries taken note of the allusion?

7. Satisfaction: does the assumption that Paul has in mind a specific text facilitate an insightful reading of the passage in which he alludes to it?[3]

While none of these criteria are decisive for determining when Paul is making an allusion to a specific text, they provide a basic mechanism to prevent readers from hearing things in Paul's letters that may not be present.

The Form(s) of the Text

Except for portions of the books of Daniel and Ezra, the Old Testament was originally written in Hebrew. Beginning in the third century BCE, Greek-speaking Jews began to translate the Hebrew Bible into Greek for the benefit of Jews who could not read it in its original language. This Greek version of the Jewish scriptures goes by the name the Septuagint (frequently abbreviated LXX in scholarly literature). Paul's letters, like the rest of the New Testament, were written in Greek. Understanding Paul's arguments when he quotes the Old Testament often depends on knowing which version he is reading.

The Septuagint rendering of most passages is straightforward. In many passages, however, the Greek and Hebrew wording differs, sometimes quite significantly. These few examples of divergent Septuagint and Hebrew texts reflect the original languages and are not due to changes made by the English translators:[4]

3. Richard B. Hays, *Echoes of Scripture in the Letters of Paul* (New Haven: Yale University Press, 1989), 29–32.

4. English translations of the Hebrew Bible are from the NRSV. English translations of the Septuagint are from Lancelot C. L. Brenton's 1851 edition, adapted by updating archaic English forms.

	Hebrew Bible (NRSV)	Greek Septuagint (Brenton)
Exod. 3:14	God said to Moses, "I AM WHO I AM."	And God spoke to Moses, saying, I am THE BEING.
Ps. 8:5	Yet you have made [humans] a little lower than God.	You made [man] a little less than angels.
Isa. 7:14	Look, the young woman is with child and shall bear a son, and shall name him Immanuel.	Behold, a virgin shall conceive in the womb, and shall bring forth a son, and you shall call his name Emmanuel.
Isa. 10:22	For though your people Israel were like the sand of the sea, only a remnant of them will return.	And though the people of Israel be as the sand of the sea, a remnant of them shall be saved.
Isa. 52:5	Their rulers howl, says the LORD, and continually, all day long, my name is despised.	On account of you my name is continually blasphemed among the Gentiles.
Hab. 2:4	The righteous live by their faith.	The just shall live by my faith.

A little more than half of Paul's Old Testament quotations are identical or nearly identical to the Septuagint text. The preference of Paul and other New Testament writers for the Septuagint is only natural given that they are writing in Greek. Nearly a third of his quotations appear in a form that matches both the Hebrew and the Greek (e.g., Gen. 17:5 in Rom. 4:17; Lev. 19:18 in Gal. 5:14; Isa. 49:8 in 2 Cor. 6:2). Almost one-quarter of his quotations agree with Septuagint wording where the Septuagint and the Hebrew text differ (e.g., Gen. 2:24 in 1 Cor. 6:16; Prov. 25:21–22 in Rom. 12:20; Isa. 54:1 in Gal. 4:27). Only a few Pauline texts quote the Old Testament in a form that agrees with the Hebrew against the Greek (e.g., Exod. 16:18 in 2 Cor. 8:15; Job 41:3 in Rom. 11:35). Finally, over 40 percent of Paul's Old Testament quotations take a form that diverges from both the Greek and the Hebrew (e.g., Gen. 2:7 in 1 Cor. 15:45; Deut. 5:16 in Eph. 6:2–3; Isa. 40:13 in 1 Cor. 2:16). The various discrepancies include differences in word order, words or phrases added or deleted, and markedly different renderings of words or phrases.

Accounting for and explaining what these discrepancies suggest about Paul as a letter writer is a bit complicated. One reason is that there were likely in circulation Hebrew manuscripts that differ from those used to produce modern translations. Another is that there were

---

The Hebrew Bible and the Old Testament

The collection of writings recognized in Judaism as authoritative or canonical goes by many different names. Christians most commonly call it the Old Testament, a term first appearing late in the second century in the works of Melito of Sardis, who may have been influenced by Paul's reference to the "old covenant" (2 Cor. 3:14). Many refer to it by the acronym *Tanak*, which stands for *Torah* (Law), *Nevi'im* (Prophets), and *Ketubim* (Writings), the three divisions of the Jewish canon. Others prefer *Miqra* ("that which is read"). Still others refer to the Masoretic Text (frequently abbreviated MT in scholarly literature), the term for the official manuscript of the Hebrew texts as they were standardized over a thousand years ago.

In recent decades, the most popular alternative to "Old Testament" is "Hebrew Bible." The Hebrew Bible and the Protestant Old Testament contain the same books, though in slightly different order. (The Catholic and Orthodox Old Testaments contain additional books that are usually labeled "Apocrypha" by Protestants and Jews.) But many regard "Hebrew Bible" as the preferable term because it avoids the imposition of a Christian theological perspective, as "Old Testament" makes sense only alongside "New Testament." Using "First Testament" and "Second Testament" is an awkward attempt at neutral terminology, with similar drawbacks. There is no perfect solution when it comes to discussing Paul's approach to the Jewish scriptures. In the sense that he relies on the Septuagint—the Greek translation of the Hebrew scriptures—Paul, it appears, rarely ever reads the Hebrew Bible.

---

multiple Greek translations of the Jewish scriptures in use. Scholars speak of "the" Septuagint for the sake of simplicity, but there was no central body in the first century dictating which Greek version was the official one and which ones were unauthorized.[5] It may also be the case that Paul is quoting from memory and is thus less precise than he would be if he had a Hebrew scroll in front of him, as is probably the case when he is writing from jail. Speakers of multiple

5. Here one may see a parallel with the proliferation of English translations of the Bible in the twentieth century. Until relatively recently, the KJV was the "official" translation for most of the English-speaking world, and its impact on language and literature was without equal. To memorize Scripture was to memorize the KJV. Two unintended effects of the wide availability of alternate translations are the loss of a shared idiom among the general public and diminished capacity to quote the Bible among those familiar with multiple versions.

languages, moreover, often alternate, consciously or unconsciously, between different forms of a familiar text.

While it is not always possible to identify the version of the Bible Paul is reading, there is frequently a clear correlation between the form of the text he quotes and the argument he is making. In Rom. 15:7–29, Paul gives advice to Jews and gentiles on how to live in harmony with one another and then tells them of his plans to travel to Spain by way of Rome to preach the gospel to the gentiles. He strings together four Old Testament quotations in 15:9–12 that relate to the gentile mission. His quotation of Isa. 11:10 in Rom. 15:12 ("the root of Jesse shall come, the one who rises to rule the Gentiles; in him the Gentiles shall hope") follows the Septuagint and thus makes the inclusion of gentiles in God's plan much more explicit than it is in the Hebrew ("the root of Jesse shall stand as a signal to the peoples; the nations shall inquire of him"). The quotation of Deut. 32:43 in Rom. 15:10 ("rejoice, O Gentiles, with his people") would make even less sense were he to quote the Hebrew (which reads in the Revised Standard Version: "Praise his people, O you nations; for he avenges the blood of his servants").

Old Testament Texts and Contexts

In his extended treatments of Abraham in Romans and of Sarah and Hagar in Galatians, Paul clearly has the original literary setting of his quotations and allusions in view and likely expects his readers to be familiar with the basic outline of the story. With briefer quotations and allusions, his cognizance of the original context is less certain. Even very diligent readers might be hard pressed to guess the context of his references to Deut. 30:12–14 in Rom. 10:5–8; to Isa. 28:11–12 in 1 Cor. 14:21; and to Ps. 116:10 in 2 Cor. 4:13. Paul recognizes as much in 1 Cor. 9:9–10, where he is defending his right as an apostle to accept material assistance from his congregation by quoting Deut. 25:4 ("you shall not muzzle an ox while it is treading out the grain"). He goes so far as to say that God in this passage "speak[s] entirely for our sake" and is not terribly concerned with oxen, as the original context seems to suggest. Paul's language is shaped by Scripture even when he is unaware of its influence. In this respect he is no different from English speakers who quote the Bible and Shakespeare without realizing it when they refer to "the writing on the wall" or "the powers that be" or describe someone as "dead as a doornail" or "pure as the driven snow."

Just as often, however, Paul's quotations and allusions reflect a conscious awareness of the original literary context from which they are taken. The reader's awareness of this setting in turn enriches their own understanding of what Paul is trying to say. He quotes Exod. 9:16 in Rom. 9:17 ("I have raised you up for the very purpose of showing my power in you, so that my name may be proclaimed in all the earth") in just such a fashion. Pharaoh is chosen not on account of or in spite of any particular moral qualities and not to be punished in hell but, rather, so that God's power might be made known. Likewise, God's election of Jews and gentiles in Rom. 9–11 is not a matter of predestining specific individuals for salvation or damnation regardless of their actions. Paul is instead asserting God's prerogative to carry out the divine plan in unexpected ways and using unwitting, even unwilling characters to do so.

Exodus supplies another example in 1 Cor. 10:1–13, which comes near the end of a discussion of meat sacrificed to idols and whether Christians should eat it. He affirms the principle that "there is no God but one" (8:4), and thus it is not really possible to commune with so-called gods by eating such meat. "We are no worse off if we do not eat," Paul says, "and no better off if we do" (8:8). Yet he also warns them not to overestimate their own wisdom or ability to resist temptation, whatever form it may take. His warning to the Corinthians to avoid idolatry includes a quotation of Exod. 32:6 in 1 Cor. 10:7 ("the people sat down to eat and drink, and they rose up to play"). This line occurs in the story of the Israelites who make the golden calf when Moses is away on Mount Sinai. The Israelites had been privileged witnesses to God's miraculous power in delivering them from Egypt and providing for their needs in the wilderness, yet they were not immune to grave spiritual error. In citing this text, Paul implies that the Corinthians, however blessed they might be with all manner of spiritual gifts, might want to err on the side of caution when it comes to even perfunctory participation in pagan rituals.

From Text to Letter, From Letter to Text

Paul justifies his use of the golden calf episode in 1 Cor. 10:11: "These things happened to them to serve as an example, and they were written down to instruct us, on whom the ends of the ages have come." His remarks underscore the two main functions of the biblical references in his letters. First, he draws on Scripture as a source of moral guidance and instruction (cf. Rom. 15:4). This may take the form of simple repetition of a statement or a command that should guide the behavior of his readers (Rom. 12:19–20; 13:9; 2 Cor. 8:15; 13:1; Gal. 5:14). Or he may direct their attention to stories and characters that serve as positive or negative examples (e.g., 1 Cor. 10:1–13).

The second function of Paul's biblical references is to support a theological argument he is making. Paul wants to communicate a number of ideas about God and Jesus and how they enter human history, in which his readers are active participants at "the ends of the ages." His explanations of these claims often rely on his interpretations of the biblical text. When he asserts in Rom. 4:1–5 that humans are justified by faith and not by works, he cites the evidence of Gen. 15:6, which says that "Abraham believed God, and it was reckoned to him as righteousness." Citing the Septuagint helps his argument more than would the Hebrew, which is not as clear on the question of who considers whom righteous in the Genesis account. Paul also interprets this as an expression of a general principle applicable to all who believe and not just a statement about Abraham and his faith in God's promise of an heir. He follows his reference to the same text in Gal. 3:6–9 with a reminder that God's original call of Abraham in Gen. 12:3 includes the promise that "all the Gentiles shall be blessed in you." The form that blessing will take is not specified. Paul interprets it as a prophecy that gentiles will become a part of the chosen people and pairs it with the example of Abraham being counted righteous centuries before the giving of the law to Moses as a precedent for accepting gentiles into the church without demanding that they abide by all Jewish laws and customs.

By what route does Paul arrive at his understanding of the texts he quotes? Many of his readings seem self-evident from a modern perspective, but this impression is occasionally a result of Paul himself decisively influencing Western thinking on the subject under consideration. At times, he starts with an idea gleaned from his earlier reading

129

of the biblical text and moves to the letter, applying the idea to a situation that presents itself. At other times, he moves in the opposite direction, from letter to the biblical text, starting with the problem prompting him to write a letter and looking back to the biblical text in search of guidance. From that same perspective, some readings seem to lack any rhyme or reason. Even here there is usually a method to his madness. In his approach to interpreting texts, Paul's methods have points of similarity as well as dissimilarity with his Jewish and non-Jewish contemporaries.

First-century Jewish interpretation of the Bible frequently focused on thorny texts and questions about their meaning, consistency with other texts, and applicability to later circumstances. Paul's education would have exposed him to the methods of the rabbis of the era. One of the most prominent of these rabbis was Hillel, who is credited with formulating a list of seven *middoth*, "rules" of inference, that reflect common interpretative practices in Paul's milieu:

1. What applies in a less important case also applies in a more important case, and vice versa (*qal wahomer*).
2. Analogous words or expressions may be applied interchangeably to two separate cases (*gezerah shavah*).
3. When a word or phrase is repeated in multiple passages, ideas associated with it are applicable in all contexts (*binyan av mekatuv ehad*).
4. A principle may be established through comparison of two passages, which may then be applied to other passages (*binyan av meshnei ketuvim*).
5. A specific regulation can be inferred where Scripture gives a general principle, and a general principle can be inferred where Scripture gives only a specific regulation (*kelal upherat*).
6. A difficulty in one passage may be resolved through comparison with a similar text (*keyitze bo' bemaqom aher*).
7. The meaning of a text may be established by its context (*davar hilamed me'inyano*).[6]

6. Cf. David Instone Brewer, *Techniques and Assumptions in Jewish Exegesis before 70 C.E.* (Tübingen: Mohr-Siebeck, 1992), 226.

Paul is not disputing with rabbis in his letters, but intellectual habits are hard to break. He does not need to name the rule he is following for scholars to recognize his use of *qal wahomer* (Rom. 5:8–11; 2 Cor. 3:7–11) and *gezerah shavah* (Rom. 4:1–12; Gal. 3:10–14), among others.

But Paul also sees limitations to the prevailing ways of reading Scripture among the Jews of his day. Jews who are not "in Christ" are like Moses with the veil over his face upon his descent from Sinai. "Indeed, to this very day," he says, "when they hear the reading of the old covenant, that same veil is still there," keeping them from understanding it rightly (2 Cor. 3:12–16). Christ is the key, and it is because his readers share his conviction that Jesus is the Messiah that Paul has confidence that they will come to understand the texts he quotes as he does.

Paul's use of the Sinai episode as an allegory for the inability of his fellow Jews to understand Torah also resembles an approach to interpreting authoritative texts taken by non-Jews in antiquity. When faced with the outrageous stories of the gods found in Homer and other myths, thoughtful Greeks and Romans frequently revert to reading them allegorically as a way of maintaining their relevance.[7] Plutarch, for example, cautions his readers not to take stories about Isis and Osiris literally but rather "reverently and philosophically," in order to grow in virtue and avoid superstitious ideas (*De Iside et Osiride* 355d). Paul removes any doubt that he might use such a strategy when he says explicitly in Gal. 4:24 that he reads the Genesis story of Sarah and Hagar and their sons Isaac and Ishmael as an allegory. Not everyone will find these approaches persuasive, but it will be difficult to make sense of what he is saying without some sense of how his arguments work in the eyes of his contemporaries.

One last observation is in order concerning the function of Paul's quotations of Scripture in his letters. History and tradition have greatly magnified Paul's voice, with the result that other first-century voices are harder to hear. But Paul is very much a part of a larger conversation taking place in his day among Jews about the meaning and

7. Luke Timothy Johnson, *Among the Gentiles: Greco-Roman Religion and Christianity* (New Haven: Yale University Press, 2009), 38.

significance of the Scriptures. Modern readers are latecomers to this conversation. For this reason, it can be difficult to discern just how much Paul and other Jews are at odds or in agreement. He spends little time or energy going over texts that present no problems. Certain ways of interpreting the Old Testament he simply takes for granted. The unintentional effect is that the differences between Paul's understanding of the Old Testament and that of other Jews appear larger than they really are. He is writing to correct perceived errors more often than to congratulate his readers on what they get right.

It would be a mistake, however, to assume that Paul's disagreements with many of his fellow Jews about the meaning of the Scriptures are nothing but unfortunate misunderstandings on his part, their part, or on the part of some modern scholars. The differences are often very real and very deep. Jesus is the Messiah according to Paul, and coming to terms with this fact is not an optional task. Faith in Jesus is nonnegotiable as a means of enjoying God's grace for Jews and gentiles alike. He does not see Christianity—were he to use that term—as Judaism for gentiles, as Franz Rosenzweig would later put it. Paul does not arrive at this unshakable belief after years of calm, detached study of the Scriptures, which led him to conclude that a fatal flaw lay at the heart of the Jewish faith. Instead, he undergoes a radical religious experience that leaves no doubt in his mind that Jesus is the pivot on which all history turns. From this conviction, he works backward to the Scriptures to understand the problem to which Jesus is the perfect solution.[8] His wrestling with Scripture in his letters, then, reveals a mind engaged in an existential quest and not a purely academic exercise.

Nonbiblical Sources

Paul's thinking is shaped by the Jewish scriptures, yet he is familiar with nonbiblical writings as well. Had he been more specific when he asked Timothy to bring him "the books, and above all the parchments"

8. E. P. Sanders writes that, for Paul, "the conviction of a universal solution preceded the conviction of a universal plight" (*Paul and Palestinian Judaism* [Minneapolis: Fortress, 1977], 474).

(2 Tim. 4:13), scholars would not have to speculate so much about his reading list. In some cases, identifying his sources poses fewer challenges. A few examples will provide a sense of the similarities and differences with his treatment of the Old Testament as well as the way in which the letter genre affects his handling of his literary sources.

In 1 Cor. 15 Paul is explaining the moral, spiritual, and even the physical significance of the resurrection. Some in Corinth are denying that there will be a resurrection of the faithful in the future. Glorified existence, they believe, is life in the present age. Paul's response is to grant their premise for the sake of argument and then to follow it to its conclusion. "If the dead are not raised," he says, "'Let us eat and drink, for tomorrow we die.' Do not be deceived: 'Bad company ruins good morals'" (15:32–33). The first quotation is from Isa. 22:13, but it echoes numerous Greek sources expressing the same thought: if death is the end, a life devoted to the pursuit of bodily pleasures makes as much sense as any other course.[9] The situation reflected elsewhere in the letter suggests that, morally speaking, some are indeed "living like there's no tomorrow." The second quotation about moral corruption is taken from a lost play by the fourth-century comic writer Menander (*Thais*, fragment 218) and reinforces the implicit warning of the first quotation. What one believes affects how one lives, according to Paul, and fraternizing with those who believe the body is of little or no ultimate import will have disastrous moral consequences.

Paul does not see Isaiah and Menander as possessing equal authority for Christians, but it is noteworthy that he sees nothing wrong with quoting them in tandem. His advice about the company they are keeping is hardly original, and he expects his readers to recognize it as common sense whether they are Jewish or gentile. Both quotations are used out of context—Isaiah is warning Jerusalem of coming destruction—yet Paul uses one to complement the other. The line from Isaiah is not an Epicurean slogan, as is often thought, but it implies a connection—that Epicurus would endorse—between a life devoted to pleasure in the here and now and the belief that personal existence ceases once and for all at death.

9. C. K. Barrett, *A Commentary on the First Epistle to the Corinthians* (London: Harper & Row, 1968), 367, cites its appearance on tombstones.

Whether it is written by Paul or someone else, the Letter to Titus also suggests a connection to Greek philosophy. The author warns his coworker about the character of the population on the island of Crete, where he has been charged with organizing a church: "It was one of them, their very own prophet, who said, 'Cretans are always liars, vicious brutes, lazy gluttons.' That testimony is true" (1:12–13). Paul clearly has a specific writer in mind. Clement of Alexandria (*Stromata* 1.59.2) first identified the source as Epimenides, a revered figure from the sixth century BCE. This quotation introduced into the letter in this manner is curious. If Cretans are always liars, and if Epimenides is a Cretan, then he must be a liar. And if he is a liar, then his statement cannot be true. On the other hand, if it is true that Cretans are always liars, then his statement corresponds to the facts and he is not lying. But this would mean that Cretans are not "always liars." So if he is lying, then he is telling the truth; and if he is telling the truth, then, as a Cretan, he must be lying. This is a paradox. In fact, it was the most famous paradox in antiquity, the Liar Paradox, discussed ad nauseam by Stoics and other philosophers (Cicero, *De finibus* 4.4.8; Plutarch, *De communibus notitiis contra Stoicos* 1070d), who were generally mocked in popular literature for their obsession with such puzzles (Athenaeus, *Deipnosophistae* 9.401e).

Why is Paul referring to, or even committing, this well-known logical fallacy? Greco-Roman treatments of the Liar Paradox show that a writer, in making a seemingly nonsensical remark, could wink at their audiences while simultaneously broaching some weightier subject. Throughout the Pastoral Epistles, the author goes to great lengths to discourage unedifying uses of speech, of which quibbling about paradoxes is but one example. Timothy is to avoid "meaningless talk" (1 Tim. 1:6) and "profane chatter and contradictions of what is falsely called knowledge" (6:20). "Wrangling over words" (2 Tim. 2:14) and "stupid and senseless controversies" (2:23; Titus 3:9) will likewise disturb the peace of the community. Irony, sarcasm, and verbal jesting of the sort one sees in Titus 1:12 are notoriously prone to misinterpretation when not accompanied by nonverbal clues such as a wink or a nudge. Given that the implied reader of the letter is a close associate, the author could reasonably expect him to get the joke.

It comes as somewhat of a surprise that Paul nowhere quotes noncanonical Jewish writings. Echoes and parallels abound, but not explicit citations of works such as *Jubilees*, *Testament of Job*, *1 Enoch*, or *Apocalypse of Zephaniah*. From the absence of direct quotations, however, one may not conclude that Paul is unfamiliar with this literature. Since he is writing letters, he is under no obligation to quote his sources fully or accurately or to include footnotes identifying his sources, as he would be were he writing a scholarly article—like the hundreds of articles devoted to identifying Paul's sources.

Conclusion

Little would remain of Paul's letters if one were to filter out the quotations and allusions to the Old Testament that they contain. Nearly every argument he makes is influenced by the Scriptures of Israel in which he is immersed. Indeed, he quotes the Old Testament far more often than he quotes Jesus. Needless to say, his proclivity for quoting the Old Testament is hardly typical of ancient letters. Paul's letters are not casual notes tossed off, like emails, with little reflection, nor are they formal treatises. They stand somewhere between these two ends of the spectrum. The letters of Jerome and Augustine, Abelard and Heloise, and Jefferson and Adams show that it is not unheard of for correspondents to focus their attention on literary or theological texts of mutual interest. Understanding how they read these shared texts is part of the process of understanding such correspondence. For Paul, reading the Old Testament and writing letters are not fundamentally separate activities. The act of writing letters to his churches drives him back to read the Scriptures. His manner of reading and interpreting the Old Testament exhibits similarities as well as dissimilarities when compared with that of his fellow Jews. How he reads the Scriptures reveals the way his mind works as he attempts to explain the significance of Jesus to his readers.

Not all of his readers would have necessarily recognized the quotations, allusions, and echoes in Paul's letters. It is inevitable that different audiences will attain different degrees of appreciation for

Paul's arguments, all the more so in light of low literacy levels in the ancient world. Christopher D. Stanley distinguishes the "informed audience," who would know the original context of Paul's quotations, from the "competent audience," who would possess the basic cultural literacy needed to grasp the point of Paul's quotations but would not know where to find them, and the "minimal audience," who would have great respect for Scripture (and for anyone who could quote it so fluently) but very little familiarity with it.[10] Any teacher knows that some students learn more from the same lesson than others. But that is not the same as saying that Paul "grossly misjudged the capacities of his audience."[11] Paul's coworkers who delivered his letters did not drop them in the mailbox and then go on their way but, rather, would likely have read them aloud to the recipients and been available to explain the significance of the references they contained. While it is often the fate of great thinkers to be misunderstood, it is questionable whether the writings of someone so rhetorically obtuse would have been saved, copied, circulated, canonized, and still studied centuries after his death.

For Further Discussion

1. Is it surprising that Paul refers to the Old Testament even in letters addressed to gentiles?
2. How does Paul's background as a Pharisaic Jew influence his reading of the Old Testament? Is he typical or atypical in his approach to the Jewish scriptures?
3. Why do Paul's quotations of Scripture sometimes match the Hebrew version (from which modern English versions are translated) but frequently diverge from it?
4. In what sense, if any, does Paul regard the Old Testament as a repository of prophecies about Jesus?

10. Christopher D. Stanley, "'Pearls before Swine': Did Paul's Audiences Understand His Biblical Quotations?" *Novum Testamentum* 41 (1999): 124–44.

11. Ibid., 133. According to Gregory of Nazianzus, "the best and most beautifully written letter is the one that is persuasive to the uneducated and educated alike" (*Epistle* 51.4).

For Further Reading

Aageson, James W. *Written Also for Our Sake: Paul and the Art of Biblical Interpretation*. Louisville: Westminster John Knox, 1993.

Beale, G. K., ed. *The Right Doctrine from the Wrong Texts? Essays on the Use of the Old Testament in the New*. Grand Rapids: Baker, 1994.

Bratcher, Robert G., ed. *Old Testament Quotations in the New Testament*. 3rd ed. New York: United Bible Society, 1984.

Ellis, E. Earle. *The Old Testament in Early Christianity: Canon and Interpretation in the Light of Modern Research*. Wissenschaftliche Untersuchungen zum Neuen Testament 54. Tübingen: Mohr, 1991.

———. *Paul's Use of the Old Testament*. Grand Rapids: Eerdmans, 1957.

Evans, C. A., and J. A. Sanders, eds. *Paul and the Scriptures of Israel*. Journal for the Study of the New Testament: Supplement Series 83. Sheffield: JSOT Press, 1993.

Hanson, A. T. *The Living Utterances of God: The New Testament Exegesis of the Old*. London: Darton, Longman & Todd, 1983.

Hays, Richard B. *The Conversion of the Imagination: Paul as Interpreter of Israel's Scripture*. Grand Rapids: Eerdmans, 2005.

———. *Echoes of Scripture in the Letters of Paul*. New Haven: Yale University Press, 1989.

Juel, Donald. *Messianic Exegesis: Christological Interpretation of the Old Testament in Early Christianity*. Philadelphia: Fortress, 1988.

Lindars, Barnabas. *New Testament Apologetic: The Doctrinal Significance of the Old Testament Quotations*. Philadelphia: Westminster, 1961.

Moyise, Steve. *The Old Testament in the New*. New York: Continuum, 2001.

———. *Paul and Scripture: Studying the New Testament Use of the Old Testament*. Grand Rapids: Baker Academic, 2010.

Mulder, Martin J. *Mikra: Text, Translation, Reading, and Interpretation of the Hebrew Bible in Ancient Judaism and Early Christianity*. Compendium Rerum Iudaicarum ad Novum Testamentum 2/1. Assen: Van Gorcum, 1988.

Porter, Stanley E., ed. *Hearing the Old Testament in the New Testament*. Grand Rapids: Eerdmans, 2006.

Porter, Stanley E., and Christopher D. Stanley, eds. *As It Is Written: Studying Paul's Use of Scripture*. Atlanta: Society of Biblical Literature, 2008.

Stanley, Christopher D. *Arguing with Scripture: The Rhetoric of Quotations in the Letters of Paul*. New York: T&T Clark, 2004.

———. *Paul and the Language of Scripture: Citation Technique in the Pauline Epistles and Contemporary Literature*. Society for New Testament Studies Monograph 69. Cambridge: Cambridge University Press, 1992.

6

⁜ ⁜ ⁜

Pseudonymity

Did Paul Write Paul's Letters?

he sum of the squares of the two shorter legs of a right triangle is equal to the square of the hypotenuse." Students of geometry know this as the Pythagorean Theorem. Although mathematicians in India and Babylon may have had knowledge of the theory before him, Pythagoras is credited as being the first to prove it. Pythagoras was an intriguing figure about whom much was written in the ancient world. He was born on the Greek island of Samos in the sixth century BCE. He established a philosophical school in Croton, located in the toe of the boot at the southern end of Italy. He advocated vegetarianism but, curiously enough, forbade his followers to eat beans.

Without this background information, is it possible to understand the Pythagorean Theorem? In a word, yes. None of it is necessary for understanding the properties of triangles. The theorem is like many other texts in this regard. Sometimes the identity of the author has little or no bearing on how one reads a text—for example, greeting cards, instructions for assembling a bookshelf, a list of Kentucky

Derby winners, a limerick, or a menu at a Chinese restaurant. At other times, it matters a great deal. Letters typically fall into this latter category. Most letters constitute a medium of communication between two parties, and thus the identity, context, and cultural assumptions of the author (as well as those of the audience) are key factors in assessing their meaning and function.

Much about Paul remains unknown to modern scholars. One thing that can be said with certainty is that Paul wrote letters. But how many did he write? Did he, and not someone else writing in his name, compose all of those attributed to him in the New Testament? The author of 2 Peter refers to a teaching of "our beloved brother Paul" and its consistency with what Paul says "in all his letters" (3:15–16). If only he had been more specific—exactly how many letters? to whom?—there would not be so much controversy about the authorship of Paul's letters as there has been for the last few centuries.

The preceding chapters have for the most part bypassed this question, one of the most fundamental to answer when one reads Paul's letters. Answering it once and for all, fortunately, is not a prerequisite for formulating strategies by which to read the letters in a manner that is attentive to historical setting and literary genre. In reality, however, most readers come to the text having already answered the authorship question, if only unconsciously. These assumptions merit close attention, for they greatly influence how one understands Paul. Readers must eventually decide whether they believe they are truly reading a letter of Paul even if the position taken is only tentative or provisional. Such presuppositions are not inappropriate—indeed, interpreting the Bible or any other text without presuppositions is impossible—but an awareness of them makes it possible to pose more astute questions and arrive at more critical insights as one reads.

This chapter will address two sets of questions. The first has to do with the main arguments in the debates about Pauline authorship: Did Paul write all of the letters attributed to him? Which ones are disputed? What types of evidence support or undermine the claims of authorship by Paul? If Paul is not the author of one or more of the letters, who is the true author? The second set of questions concerns the larger significance of the debate: Does it really matter whether Paul wrote "Paul's letters"? For whom does it matter? What are the implications of recognizing or denying that someone else may have been responsible for composing letters in the apostle's name?

The Question of Authenticity

Thirteen letters in the New Testament purport to be from Paul. Doubts about their authorship are rare before the eighteenth century. Scholars have called into question the authorship of each of these letters over the last few centuries. A very broad consensus has nevertheless developed concerning which letters are from Paul and which letters were written by someone else. The seven *undisputed* letters, sometimes referred to as the authentic or genuine letters, are these:

Romans	Philippians
1 Corinthians	1 Thessalonians
2 Corinthians	Philemon
Galatians	

The six *disputed* letters, sometimes referred to as the inauthentic, deutero-Pauline, or pseudo-Pauline letters, are these:

Ephesians
Colossians
2 Thessalonians
Pastoral Epistles: 1 Timothy, 2 Timothy, Titus

A sizable minority of scholars believe that 2 Thessalonians and Colossians belong among the authentic letters. Arguments for including Ephesians among the authentic letters find less traction. The Pastoral Epistles, which many believe were written several decades after Paul's death, enjoy very little support.

On what basis have scholars arrived at this consensus? The debate typically turns on three factors. First, when the information about Paul's missionary activity supplied by a given letter is not consistent with the itinerary found in the Acts of the Apostles—the earliest narrative account of Paul's travels—then that letter's claim to authenticity is deemed suspect. For example, the author of the Letter to Titus (1:5)

141

Hebrews among the Letters of Paul

Many older editions of the English Bible include "The Epistle of Paul the Apostle to the Hebrews," but the letter itself—apart from this superscription—nowhere names Paul as its author. Hebrews is anonymous, not pseudonymous. For this reason, in addition to the differences in style and theology between Hebrews and other letters bearing Paul's name that were noted in antiquity, scholars exclude Hebrews from the corpus of Pauline literature.

Over the centuries, the many names put forward as the likely author of Hebrews comprise a veritable "who's who" of the early church: Luke, Stephen, Barnabas, Apollos, Priscilla, and the Virgin Mary. Barring some unforeseen discovery, the best answer to the question of the authorship of Hebrews will remain Origen's in the third century: "God knows."

---

addresses a situation in the church at Crete, yet Paul hardly has time to plant a church on the island on his sea journey to Rome as described in Acts 27. First Corinthians and 1 Thessalonians, by contrast, fit perfectly within the framework of the Acts narrative and are universally accepted as genuine. This criterion does not yield definitive evidence against the disputed letters since Acts does not offer an exhaustive account of Paul's career. Insofar as many scholars lack confidence in its accuracy, moreover, it is perhaps problematic to use Acts by itself as a standard by which to judge claims of authorship.

Second, differences in the style of writing, including syntax, word choice, and rhetorical strategy, provide stronger evidence against the authenticity of the disputed letters. Especially telling are the differences in vocabulary, including a high percentage of *hapax legomena*.[1] Colossians, a relatively short document, contains eighty-seven words found nowhere else in the undisputed letters, twenty-five found nowhere else in any of the letters, and thirty-four found nowhere else in the New Testament, with sentence lengths that are longer than what one usually sees in Paul. Of the approximately eight hundred words used in the Pastoral Epistles, 175 are *hapax legomena*; and three hundred words appear nowhere else in any of the letters attributed to Paul. "Faith" and "law" seem to have meanings not typically attached

---

1. A *hapax legomenon* (plural, *hapax legomena*) is any word that appears only once in the New Testament.

to those terms in Paul's other letters. The language and style of the Pastorals, it is also argued, resembles that of Hellenistic philosophical writings. The style found in 1 Timothy and Titus in particular is in key respects closer to that of Luke-Acts than to that of Romans or Galatians.

Defenders of the disputed letters contend that statistical analyses of word usage are often unreliable, particularly when the sample size is relatively small. The results would be much more trustworthy with a more prolific letter writer like Cicero, John Adams, or Johnny Cash, who sent hundreds of letters to his fiancée over a three-year period when he was stationed in Germany with the US Air Force. Vocabulary, tone, and syntax, moreover, naturally change when the audience, occasion, and subject matter change. Paul's audiences include rich and poor, Jew and gentile, groups recently converted and groups with deeper roots in the faith, churches Paul founded and churches he has never visited, and individuals with whom he is at odds as well as his most trusted colleagues. Given such varied audiences and reasons for writing, it would be surprising to encounter a single, consistent style, as Cicero remarks in one of his own letters (*Epistulae ad familiares* 9.21.1). To draw a modern parallel, it would be difficult to discern the same hand at work if all one possessed were a student's term

---

Measuring Style

Paul joins a long list of authors whose works have been subjected to stylometric analysis. Stylometry is a statistical method for measuring various aspects of linguistic style, often for the purpose of determining authorship. Developed in the nineteenth century, it became more widely used with the advent of computers.[1] Homer, Plato, James Joyce, C. S. Lewis, Barack Obama, and the Unabomber have all received stylometric scrutiny, as have the Qur'an, the Book of Mormon, and the Hitler Diaries. Its practitioners concede that it is an imperfect science. One scholar used computer-aided analysis to "prove" that Francis Bacon wrote several of Shakespeare's plays, but another scholar used the same techniques to "prove" that Bacon also wrote Caesar's *Gallic Wars*, Spenser's *Faerie Queene*, the King James Version of the Bible, Longfellow's *Hiawatha*, Melville's *Moby-Dick*, and the *Federalist Papers*.

1. David I. Holmes, "The Evolution of Stylometry in Humanities Scholarship," *Literary and Linguistic Computing* 13 (1998): 111–17.

paper for a history class, a note to her grandmother, an essay on a scholarship application, a letter to a pen pal in France, an email to a close friend, and a condolence card to an acquaintance whose father has passed away.

In addition, Paul uses an amanuensis or secretary in at least one of his letters (Romans) and possibly several others. Secretaries in the Greco-Roman world acted not only as scribes taking dictation but frequently had considerable freedom to edit or even compose letters on behalf of their employers.[2] Seven of the letters, finally, mention by name a cosender or coauthor in the opening verses. The effect of Paul's relationship with his coauthors upon the precise wording of the letters may be similar to the example of a president and speechwriter, such as John F. Kennedy and Ted Sorenson. It is said of Sorenson that he "knew where Kennedy stood and he could phrase what Kennedy's ideas were better than Kennedy could himself."[3] Without more precise knowledge of the involvement of Timothy, Silvanus, Sosthenes, Tertius, and others in the process of composition, arguments from style remain inconclusive (see appendix 2).

Third, inconsistency in theme or theological teaching is perhaps the most compelling evidence that Paul did not write the disputed letters. It is difficult to reconcile Paul's commitment to equality in Christ (Gal. 3:28–29) and the authority he grants to such women as Phoebe, Chloe, and Priscilla with the perspective of 1 Tim. 2:11–12, where the author states that a woman should "learn in silence with full submission" and that he does not permit women "to teach or to have authority over a man." The idea that women "will be saved by childbearing" (2:15) seems at odds with the doctrine of justification by faith (Gal. 2:16). Mention of specific signs preceding the second coming in 2 Thess. 2 is thought to run counter to the notion in 1 Thess. 5:2 that Jesus's return will be unexpected, "like a thief in the night." And whereas Ephesians describes marriage as a mystical sign of the

2. Jerome Murphy-O'Connor, *Paul the Letter-Writer: His World, His Options, His Skills* (Collegeville, MN: Michael Glazier/Liturgical Press, 1995), 6–19; and E. Randolph Richards, *Paul and First-Century Letter Writing: Secretaries, Composition, and Collection* (Downers Grove, IL: InterVarsity, 2004), 59–80.

3. Robert Schlesinger, *White House Ghosts: Presidents and Their Speechwriters* (New York: Simon & Schuster, 2008), 142.

relationship between Christ and the church (5:22–33), in 1 Cor. 7 Paul appears to regard it as an arrangement in place only for those unable to restrain their passions.

These differences have been exaggerated in the view of many scholars, who have attempted to account for the apparent contradictions that inevitably result when modern audiences eavesdrop on ancient conversations not intended for their ears. Anyone privy to the original context and occasion would not see any inconsistency at all. Others defend the disputed letters by suggesting that Paul's thinking on certain issues undergoes development over his career; put differently, Paul changes his mind. It may also be that Paul is simply human, and all humans are inconsistent at some time or other. This solution may salvage Pauline authorship for the disputed letters while creating a separate problem for those who view Scripture as inerrant.

Not all scholars place equal weight on the same factors, nor is there universal agreement about the implications of the evidence even among those who maintain similar views on the question of authorship. This overview of the issues involved, however brief, provides some sense of the assumptions and concerns of Paul's past and present readers.

Does It Matter Whether Paul Wrote "Paul's Letters"?

Is all the sound and fury over the authorship of Paul's letters much ado about nothing? Does it or should it affect how one reads the New Testament? There are two basic dimensions to the question, the theological and the literary-historical.

Had the early church not included Paul's letters in its canon of Scripture, it is likely that very few people over the last two thousand years would have read any of them. Even today, most of Paul's readers regard his writings as authoritative texts to be consulted for guidance on matters of moral and spiritual import. Does the debate about authorship influence how these readers approach the letters? For many, yes, it makes a considerable difference. If Paul is not the author of the writings that bear his name, then they are in some sense illegitimate. Many early theologians explicitly argued that they merited inclusion on account of the special authority of their author, and many modern readers are inclined to agree. For others, the controversy is of little consequence. It is sufficient that the disputed letters are in the canon, and they merit study for that reason alone. The church canonized texts, not persons. What matters is the message, not the messenger, even if the church decided to include certain texts by mistake, so to speak, thinking that they were from Paul when they were penned by someone else.[4]

Whether or in what way Paul's putative authorship *ought to* influence the way Christians read the letters is an important theological question but it is beyond the scope of this book. This theological discussion is nevertheless informed by the results of literary-historical investigation.

Are debates about the identity of the author relevant to the larger task of understanding the letters from a purely historical or literary perspective? Interpreters at opposite ends of the spectrum with respect to the authorship of the disputed letters agree that the answer is yes. To a higher degree than is true with most other genres, the role of the author is a critical factor in the interpretation of epistolary literature. Reading a letter necessarily involves the attempt to discern the author's purposes as well as the reception the letter was likely to receive from its original or intended audience. Because letters—Paul's, at any rate—purport to be from a specific individual to a (more or less) specific audience, it is essential to have a working hypothesis about the intended function of the salutation, greetings, personal references, and the like.

Either Paul wrote the letters attributed to him or someone else did. If Paul did not write one or more of these letters, then someone wrote them under a pseudonym. On this assumption, one must then ask: If someone else wrote, say, Colossians, did that author act with the understanding and the desire that his audience would see through the pseudonym as a transparent fiction? What aim did the author hope to accomplish by posing as Paul? Would the recipients of the letter regard that aim as straightforward and unproblematic, or would it have the taint of impropriety? (See appendix 2.)

4. Discomfort with the idea of anonymous authorship is not peculiar to theologically oriented readers. Jack Stillinger likens it to the experience of sitting through a symphony or touring a gallery without knowing the names of the composer or the artists; see *Multiple Authorship and the Myth of Solitary Genius* (New York: Oxford University Press, 1991), 186.

Pseudonymous authorship was widely practiced in Jewish and Greco-Roman antiquity. It is not uncommon to find writings ascribed to revered figures from the distant past such as Adam, Enoch, Shem, Elijah, Homer, Orpheus, Pythagoras, and Socrates. In certain genres it was a standard convention to use a false name, and it would not have been deemed inappropriate in its original context because there was no intent to deceive and the convention was understood by all parties. According to many scholars, the disputed letters belong to this class of writings. In fact, the practice was one way of honoring an illustrious personage by perpetuating his spirit and teaching for a new time and place.[5]

The disputed letters are thought to be the product of a Pauline school operating in this fashion, making use in some cases of authentic fragments from Paul's own hand. Neo-Pythagorean writers followed this custom, according to the philosopher Iamblichus. But it would be a mistake to read the Socratic epistles, for example, in the hope of learning about Socrates firsthand or about conditions in fifth-century BCE Athens. Such documents shed light instead on the later context in which they were composed. In the same way, it may be that the tone of the author's comments about Jews and gentiles in Eph. 2–3 and the apparent conflict over the treatment of widows in 1 Tim. 5 reflect the circumstances of communities at the beginning of the second century rather than during Paul's lifetime. Recognizing that these documents may have been written by someone other than the supposed author is one key to their proper interpretation.

On the other hand, this approach may overlook evidence of a different attitude. Galen, a famous second-century CE physician, was greatly displeased to see medical treatises published in his name in Rome and even wrote a book on how to tell a fake from the real thing. Herodotus says that one Onomacritus was expelled from Athens for writing and inserting forged material into the oracles of Musaeus.

---

5. James D. G. Dunn employs the analogy of a painting from the studio of a great master: "While the brush-strokes may not have been made by the master himself, . . . the character and quality and inspiration of the work can properly be said to be his, even when the work was conceived and executed after his death" ("Pseudepigraphy," in *Dictionary of the Later New Testament and Its Developments*, ed. R. P. Martin and P. H. Davids [Downers Grove, IL: InterVarsity, 1997], 984).

Epicureans like Philodemus of Gadara labored to ensure that spurious works were not falsely attributed to the founders of their school, as did Peripatetic philosophers such as Andronicus of Rhodes for the works of Aristotle.[6] Whatever the motive—financial, political, philosophical, or personal—these cases demonstrate that the view of pseudonymity as a benign practice did not extend to every instance.[7] Be it Paul or someone else, the author of 2 Thessalonians confirms this when he admonishes his readers "not to be quickly shaken in mind or alarmed, either by spirit or by word *or by letter, as though from us*, to the effect that the day of the Lord is already here. *Let no one deceive you in any way*" (2:2–3, emphasis added).

Would Paul approve of a Pauline school? Paul is neither the first nor the last writer to die without tying up every loose end. Great writers are often prickly when it comes to other eyes seeing their manuscripts or having their name attached to the work of someone else. (And many not-so-great writers might be appalled at the idea of their private letters being published for all the world to see.) Some, like Albert Einstein, J. R. R. Tolkien, and Ludwig Wittgenstein, appoint literary executors whom they trust to make decisions about handling their work and managing their "brand" after they are gone. But such wishes are not always respected. According to legend, the Roman poet Virgil died before finishing his masterpiece, *The Aeneid*, and on his deathbed requested that the manuscript be burned. Franz Kafka, Emily Dickinson, and Vladimir Nabokov made similar—and similarly ignored—requests.

Figuring out what an author *would have* wanted or *would have* said is a tricky business. (Thirty years after Nabokov's death, though, his son had a convenient solution: he reports that his father appeared in a vision granting permission to publish his final novel.) It becomes

6. See H. Gregory Snyder, *Teachers and Texts in the Ancient World: Philosophers, Jews, and Christians* (London: Routledge, 2000), 51–52, 66–74. The mere idea of a student circulating versions of his works without permission—to say nothing of the prospect of others "borrowing" his name for their own compositions—was enough to raise the hackles of first-century CE Roman rhetorician Quintilian (*Institutio oratoria* 1 pr. 7–8).

7. Bruce M. Metzger, "Literary Forgeries and Canonical Pseudepigrapha," *Journal of Biblical Literature* 91 (1972): 3–24. "Indeed," Metzger notes, "if nobody was taken in by the device of pseudepigraphy, it is difficult to see why it was adopted at all" (16).

even trickier when fame—or infamy—comes as a result of posthumous publications. Friedrich Nietzsche, for example, was a favorite of Hitler's. Would Nietzsche have seen Hitler as a kindred spirit? Or was Nazi sympathy for his thought a result of his sister Elisabeth's questionable editing of his unpublished writings? Would Paul read the works of his followers with approval, or would he declare, like J. Alfred Prufrock, "That is not what I meant at all"?

Conclusion

There is no one-size-fits-all solution when it comes to determining how to read the disputed letters. Each writing presents its own distinctive set of problems. It is perhaps more difficult to accept 2 Thessalonians as a harmless fiction if it is not by Paul than 2 Timothy, Titus,

---

An Illustrious Correspondent

Jefferson and Adams. Freud and Jung. Barrett and Browning. The annals of letter writing include numerous pairs of famous pen pals. Before all these, there was Paul and Seneca.

Lucius Annaeus Seneca was a Roman philosopher and politician who served as tutor and, later, advisor to Nero. He was a prolific writer of essays, letters, and plays. When Nero suspects him of conspiracy, he orders Seneca to commit suicide, quite possibly in the same year that, according to tradition, he has Paul beheaded. In their fourteen letters the two men form a mutual admiration society, though Seneca expresses more admiration for Paul, whose letters are "so lofty and so brilliant with noble sentiments."

The only problem is that the correspondence is fake.[1] It resembles the modern phenomenon of "ghost-letters," an exercise used by creative-writing teachers in which students compose letters to and from renowned figures from history and literature. The letters are artifacts of a time when, a few centuries after their deaths, both men had become well known. Perhaps the inspiration came from the similarities some saw between Paul's teachings and Seneca's Stoic philosophy (see Tertullian, *De anima* 20). The correspondence planted a seed that bloomed in the Middle Ages, when it was widely believed that the apostle had converted the philosopher to Christianity.

1. The full correspondence may be found in J. K. Elliott, *The Apocryphal New Testament* (Oxford: Oxford University Press, 2005), 547–53.

---

or Ephesians. All hypotheses about authorial intent or anticipated reception must be tested against the information gleaned from a close reading of the text, and the danger of circular reasoning is always present when so many variables remain uncertain.

As with other genres, audience expectation is a crucial consideration. Theodor Geisel was able to write as "Dr. Seuss," confident that no one would be upset upon learning that he had never attended medical school. Likewise, when a church newsletter prints a "letter from Jesus" on the topic of "taking Christ out of Christmas," even small children recognize it for what it is. It is one thing to ascribe an apocalyptic vision to a figure from the hoary past like Abraham or Ezra, but perhaps something very different to write a letter to a specific audience and sign it with the name of a controversial contemporary. By the late first century when the disputed letters are thought to have been written, is Paul more like the former, as he is in the apocryphal correspondence between Paul and the Roman Stoic Seneca, or the latter, a lightning rod whose invocation might ignite as many quarrels as it would settle?

For Further Discussion

1. Which of the arguments against the Pauline authorship of the disputed letters are the strongest? Which are the weakest?
2. How does consideration of genre factor into discussions of Pauline authorship?
3. One's position on the question of authorship affects interpretation in obvious ways. Are there any respects in which one's interpretation remains the same whether Paul or someone else is the author of a letter?
4. If Paul is not the author of one or more of the disputed letters, what purpose(s) might be served by the use of the pseudonym?

For Further Reading

Aland, Kurt. "The Problem of Anonymity and Pseudonymity in Christian Literature of the First Two Centuries." *Journal of Theological Studies* 12 (1961): 39–49.

Carson, D. A. "Pseudonymity and Pseudepigraphy." In *Dictionary of New Testament Background*, edited by C. A. Evans and S. E. Porter, 857–64. Downers Grove, IL: InterVarsity, 2000.

Collins, Raymond F. *Letters That Paul Did Not Write: The Epistle to the Hebrews and the Pauline Pseudepigrapha*. Wilmington, DE: Liturgical Press, 1988.

Dunn, James D. G. "Pauline Legacy and School." In *Dictionary of the Later New Testament and Its Developments*, edited by R. P. Martin and P. H. Davids, 887–93. Downers Grove, IL: InterVarsity, 1997.

———. "Pseudepigraphy." In *Dictionary of the Later New Testament and Its Developments*, edited by R. P. Martin and P. H. Davids, 977–84. Downers Grove, IL: InterVarsity, 1997.

Ellis, E. Earle. "Pseudonymity and Canonicity of New Testament Documents." In *Worship, Theology, and Ministry in the Early Church*, edited by M. J. Wilkins and T. Paige, 212–24. Sheffield: Sheffield Academic Press, 1992.

Harrison, P. N. *The Problem of the Pastoral Epistles*. London: Oxford University Press, 1921.

Johnson, Luke T. *The Writings of the New Testament: An Interpretation*. Rev. ed. Minneapolis: Fortress, 1999.

Meade, D. G. *Pseudonymity and Canon: An Investigation into the Relationship of Authorship and Authority in Jewish and Earliest Christian Tradition*. Wissenschaftliche Untersuchungen zum Neuen Testament 39. Tübingen: Mohr, 1986.

Metzger, Bruce M. "Literary Forgeries and Canonical Pseudepigrapha." *Journal of Biblical Literature* 91 (1972): 3–24.

Richards, E. Randolph. *Paul and First-Century Letter Writing: Secretaries, Composition, and Collection*. Downers Grove, IL: InterVarsity, 2004.

———. *The Secretary in the Letters of Paul*. Wissenschaftliche Untersuchungen zum Neuen Testament 2.42. Tübingen: Mohr-Siebeck, 1991.

Wilder, Terry L. *Pseudonymity, the New Testament, and Deception: An Inquiry into Intention and Reception*. Lanham, MD: University Press of America, 2004.

Epilogue

Beyond Paul

P aul gets the lion's share of the attention of scholars and non-specialists alike, for a variety of historical and cultural reasons, but he was not the only person to write letters in the first century or so of Christian history. In addition to the disputed letters that purport to be by Paul but may have been written by someone else, the New Testament contains the anonymous Letter to the Hebrews, the Letter of James, 1–2 Peter, 1–3 John, and the Letter of Jude. Other letters were surely written but have not survived. All too often these letters are ignored or dismissed as marginal, irrelevant, or unworthy of inclusion in the canon. Martin Luther, for example, relegated Hebrews, James, and Jude to the appendix of his German translation of the New Testament. Even when these texts are studied, they are frequently compared to the Pauline "standard" of what a letter ought to be. (It is uncertain whether this marginalization of the non-Pauline letters is a result—or a cause—of the scholarly consensus that each of these letters is pseudonymous.) A brief overview of these letters will serve as a closing reminder that Paul is best read against the backdrop of a much larger epistolary landscape and not the other way around, that is, that ancient letters should be read through the prism of Paul's letters.

153

Hebrews resembles a sermon as much as a letter. It closes with epistolary greetings, leading some scholars to hypothesize that the final chapter was added to an otherwise stand-alone homily. Continuity in theme and language, however, strongly suggest that all thirteen chapters were meant to go together. The author, whose Greek style is perhaps the finest in the New Testament, seeks to emphasize the finality of God's revelation in Jesus (1:1–3). He exhorts his readers, who have undergone some form of persecution (10:32–34), to follow the example of Jesus in persevering through hard times (12:1–3), to press on toward perfection (6:1–2; 10:38–39), and to avoid the fate of those who fall away (2:1–3; 3:7–4:11; 6:4–6; 10:19–31). These objectives qualify the letter as a specimen of deliberative rhetoric, though the glorification of Jesus in comparison with the angels, Moses, and the levitical priests exhibits elements of epideictic rhetoric, as does the lengthy roll call of the heroes and heroines of faith in Heb. 11.

The Letter of James is addressed to "the twelve tribes in the Dispersion" (1:1). James was one of the most common names among Jews in the first century, but most scholars believe that the brother of Jesus is the implied author. The content of the letter is reminiscent of Jewish Wisdom literature like Proverbs and Sirach. At a number of points the parenesis of which it largely consists echoes teachings of Jesus (James 1:4; 2:5; 4:9–10; 5:1, 12), of whom there is barely any mention. Use of the diatribe is seen in a number of sections, most notably in the discussion of faith and works (2:14–26), which draws frequent comparison with Paul's letters to the Romans and the Galatians.

First Peter is sent from "Babylon" (5:13), likely a code word for Rome, to "exiles" in the Roman province of Asia (1:1). Although some see it as a baptismal homily parading as a letter, 1 Peter appears to address a real, if general, audience facing the prospect of persecution (2:22–23; 3:9–12; 4:12–19). The author urges the readers to live godly lives and to "be ready to make your defense to anyone who demands from you an accounting for the hope that is in you . . . with gentleness and reverence" (3:15–16). Toward this end, as Paul instructs the Romans, the gentile audience is told to honor the imperial authorities (1 Pet. 2:13–17). Other similarities with Pauline writings include the household code found in 2:18–3:7.

Second Peter is intended for a general audience. Its genre appears to be that of "testament" or "farewell discourse." As with other testaments in Jewish literature, one finds warnings about false teachers (2:1–3, 10–22; 3:1–4) and exhortations to godly living (3:11–17). Parallels with the Letter of Jude suggest that it may have been used as a source by the author of 2 Peter. This, along with the concern about the apparent delay of the second coming (3:8: "with the Lord one day is like a thousand years, and a thousand years are like one day"), leads many scholars to believe that 2 Peter is the latest composition in the New Testament.

First John exhibits relatively few epistolary features, yet it appears to address a real theological crisis threatening the audience. The author alternates between exposition and exhortation. His chief concern is to counter those who deny that Jesus has come in the flesh (4:1–3). This error coincides with a distressing lack of love in the community (2:9–11; 4:7–12). More than any other documents in the New Testament, 2 John and 3 John resemble ordinary Hellenistic letters in terms of form and length. The former warns "the elect lady and her children"—probably a small house church—not to extend hospitality to heretics. The latter commends "beloved Gaius" for his hospitality and upbraids a certain Diotrophes for his lack of hospitality.

The Letter of Jude is addressed simply to "those who are called." The author identifies himself as the brother of James, which implies that he is also the brother of Jesus. The aim of this short letter is to encourage the audience "to contend for the faith" against certain individuals who are teaching "licentiousness" (3–4). Of special note is the way in which the author quotes or alludes to noncanonical works such as *1 Enoch* and *Life of Moses*.

Each of these letters shows similarities and differences when compared to Paul's writings, as do those of Clement of Rome, Ignatius of Antioch, and Polycarp of Smyrna only a few decades later. But the same strategies may be applied in order to understand them. Asking the right questions facilitates a more responsible, incisive way of interpreting the various dimensions of these letters. Familiarity with the cultural context will make it easier to detect the assumptions shared by the author and the original audience. Identifying the specific epistolary genres in which they write will help modern readers see more clearly what they are (and are not) trying to accomplish. The standard ways of organizing letters alert readers to the rhetorical aspects of the arguments they contain. Inquiring about the intended audience generates details that bring the author's arguments into clearer focus, as does following up on the other texts he quotes and expects his readers to recognize. To borrow a phrase from Paul, modern readers of ancient Christian letters "see through a glass darkly," but attention to these and other factors brings much-needed light.

Appendix 1

Dating Paul's Letters

W hile there is a very general consensus about the time frame in which Paul wrote his surviving letters, significant differences remain. This chart provides a representative sample of the range of dates suggested by critical scholars (sources are listed in the bibliography).

	Robinson	Holladay	Gorman	Jewett	Lüdemann	Meeks and Fitzgerald	Bruce
Romans	57	57–58	late 50s	56–57	51–52	ca. 57	57
1 Corinthians	55	54–55	mid-50s	55	49	53–55	55–56
2 Corinthians	56	56–57	mid-50s	55–56	50	54–56	55–56
Galatians	56	54–55	early to mid-50s	52–54	50	ca. 54	48?
Ephesians	58	ca. 70–90	60s (or later?)	*	*	ca. 80	60–62?
Philippians	58	54–55	mid-late 50s	54–55	*	ca. 62? 56?	60–62?
Colossians	58	61–63	early 60s?	55–56	*	65–75?	60–62?
1 Thessalonians	50	51–52	late 40s/very early 50s	46–51	41	50–51	50
2 Thessalonians	50–51	51–52	early 50s (or later)	46–51	*	ca. 51	50
1 Timothy	55	ca. 70–90	after Paul's death?	*	*	95–125?	65?
2 Timothy	58	ca. 70–90	early 60s?	*	*	95–125?	65?
Titus	57	ca. 70–90	after Paul's death?	*	*	95–125?	65?
Philemon	58	61–63	50s	55–56	*	ca. 62? 56?	60–62?

*No date assigned.

For Further Reading

Bruce, F. F. *Paul: Apostle of the Free Spirit*. Exeter: Paternoster, 1977. Published in the US under the title *Paul: Apostle of the Heart Set Free*. Rev. ed. Carlisle, UK: Paternoster; Grand Rapids: Eerdmans, 2000.

Gorman, Michael J. *Reading Paul*. Eugene, OR: Cascade, 2008.

Holladay, Carl R. *A Critical Introduction to the New Testament: Interpreting the Message and Meaning of Jesus Christ*. Nashville: Abingdon, 2005.

Jewett, Robert. *A Chronology of Paul's Life*. Philadelphia: Fortress, 1979.

Lüdemann, Gerd. *Paul, Apostle to the Gentiles: Studies in Chronology*. Translated by F. S. Jones. Philadelphia: Fortress, 1984.

Meeks, Wayne A., and John T. Fitzgerald, eds. *The Writings of St. Paul*. 2nd ed. New York: Norton, 2007.

Robinson, J. A. T. *Redating the New Testament*. Philadelphia: Westminster, 1978.

Appendix 2

Defining Authorship

What does it mean when we refer to someone as the author of a text? It may seem like this question has a simple answer, but when one considers the various ways in which texts are produced, it becomes clear that the matter is not always so straightforward. Consider the examples described below. Who deserves to be called the "author"? Is there any moral or ethical dimension to the scenario that should be considered?

a. A public relations employee of a business writes a letter for the business. After the president of the company reads and approves the letter, it is sent out with the company president's signature on it.

b. A public relations employee creates a quotation for a press release and attributes it to another employee of the company. After approval by the cited employee, the press release is distributed with the "quotation."

Adapted from Scott Shauf, "Authorship and Pseudonymity," in *Teaching the Bible: Practical Strategies for Classroom Instruction*, ed. M. Roncace and P. Gray, Resources for Biblical Study 49 (Atlanta: Society of Biblical Literature, 2005), 354–56.

c. A preacher delivers a sermon found in a published book of sermons. The preacher makes no statement about the source of the sermon.

d. Someone writes a book using a pen name. The pen name makes it appear that the author is of a different gender, ethnicity, or nationality from the author's actual gender, ethnicity, or nationality.

e. A politician delivers a speech expressing the politician's views on a public policy issue. The speech is actually written by an employed speechwriter.

f. A journalist writes an article for a magazine. The editor makes numerous stylistic changes and cuts much of the content of the article before publishing it.

g. Church member X is asked to write an amendment to be made to the church bylaws. Member X thinks member Y would do a better job and asks Y to do it instead. Y agrees, but because of Y's controversial reputation, Y doesn't want Y's name associated with the writing. Therefore X and Y agree that Y will write the document, but X will present it without any indication that Y was involved.

h. A scientist has a stroke and becomes unable to work after having completed the research and analysis of an important experiment. Some students of the scientist gather all of his notes, and then write up and publish the scientist's findings in the scientist's name.

i. A well-known scholar is asked to contribute to a volume of essays on the Civil War. The essay she produces consists largely of paragraphs drawn from earlier books she had written on related topics. When writing the earlier books, she had received help from student research assistants.

Such examples are not uncommon, and many are analogous to various proposals for authorship for Paul's letters.

General Index

Scripture and Ancient Sources Index